# HORSE TRAILS
OF
OKLAHOMA

by Betty Robinson

EQUESTRIAN UNLTD., INC. • LONDON, ARKANSAS

© 1997 by Equestrian Unltd., Inc.
London, Arkansas

All rights reserved, including the right to reproduce parts or sections of this book in any form, except for inclusion of brief quotations in a review.

Printed in the United States of America.

Photographs by Betty Robinson and Pat Gordon.

Maps by Justin Stokes

Illustrations by Becky Garner

Library of Congress Catalog Card Number: 97-060877.

ISBN 0-929183-05-3

Equestrian Unltd., Inc.
P.O. Box 255
London, AR 72847-0255

Additional copies of this book may be purchased from
Tack 'N Trails USA
P.O. Box 255
London, AR 72847-0255

Contents

Acknowledgments	v
Caution	vii
Introduction	ix
About the Oklahoma Equestrian Trail Riders Association	xiii
Oklahoma Horse Trails Map	xv
Map Legend	xvi

Oklahoma - Northwest

Oklahoma-Northwest Map	2
Black Kettle National Grasslands	3
Coyote Hills Ranch	6
Foss Lake Equestrian Trails	8
Roman Nose Horse Trails	10
Salt Plains Horse Trails	13

Oklahoma - Northeast

Oklahoma-Northeast Map	16
Cherokee Gruber Wildlife Management Area	17
Camp Wah-Shah-She Horse Trail	20
Rocky Bluff Horse Trail	22
Bell Cow Horse Trails	25
Five Fingers Equestrian Trail	29
Horsethief Canyon	33
Jean Pierre Chouteau Trail	35
Lake Carl Blackwell Equestrian Trails	41
Okmulgee Wildlife Management Area	43
Walnut Creek Equine Trails	46
Will Rogers Country Centennial Trail	50

Oklahoma - Southeast

Oklahoma-Southeast Map	56
Billy Creek Trail	57
Cedar Lake Equestrian Trails	61
Chickasaw National Recreation Horse Trails	67
Honobia Horse Trails	71
Horse Pen Trail	73
Indian Hills Ranch Horse Trails	75
Indian Mounds Horse Trails	78
Lake Murray Field Trial Horse Trails	81
Platter-Lakeside Equestrian Trails	84
Lexington Wildlife Management Area	88
Little River Boomtown Trails	90
McGee Creek Natural Scenic Recreation Horse Trails	93
Robbers Cave Equestrian Trails	97
Sportsman Lake Equestrian Trails	101
Stanley Draper Lake Horse Trail	104
Talimena Horse Trails	106

Oklahoma - Southwest

Oklahoma-Southwest Map	112
Sandy Sanders Wildlife Management Area	113
Walker Creek Equestrian Trail	116

State Park Stables 120

Guest Ranches 123

About Our Illustrator 126

About the Author 128

About the Cover Photographs

Pat Gordon chose the photographs for the cover because of their representation of the land, history, and people of Oklahoma. The back cover photos were taken at (top to bottom) Wichita Mountain Wildlife Refuge, Coyote Hills Ranch, and Tall Grass Prairie Reserve. The front cover demonstrates today's true western look.

Acknowledgments

Three years ago this book was a dream. Two years ago it became a pain in my back-side. Last year it grew to a challenge. I began to wonder if I could really do it. This year, 8500 plus trailer miles later, the book is finally complete.

When you start a project like this you never know what lies ahead. As expected, there are always good things and things not so good. Throughout this experience one good thing I could count on consistently, was the friendship and support of the Oklahoma Trail Riders. These riders met me at trailheads, shared their food, put up with my cantankerous mule Dr. Ruth, and even provided a hot shower and soft bed when I didn't think I could drive another mile. It never seems appropriate to pick out a few people to thank when so many had a part in the success of the project, but you just have to thank a few.

First, I would like to thank my computer support, Sylvia Rogers and Anne Burnsed. No matter how many stupid or repetitive questions I had they always managed to get back to me with some kind of an answer.

Second, I want to thank riders who shared specific trails with me. Louise Burton for sharing the Panther Prowl trails in the Okmulgee WLMA. Vicky Carnahan who rode with me at Walnut Creek State Park. Terry and Debi Casey, Clayton Dean, Keith Coleman, Becky and Dave McHahen for riding with me at Robber's Route. Pete and Cathy House for sharing their home and their trails at Little River Boomtown. Grant and Deanna Hodges for sharing their home, some of the best BBQ in northern Oklahoma, and the Five Finger Equestrian trails at Kaw Lake. Paula and David Grimes for sharing Sportsman Equestrian Trails at Seminole. Jess Johnson at Indian Mounds Campgrounds for not only sharing the trails, but for also taking me back out to find my easy boot and getting me a farrier in an emergency. Ivone Nail for her work on trails all around Oklahoma and most especially for sharing the new trails at Talimena State Park. To Jackie Walker, her granddaughter, Tara

Walker and Mike Boren for a fun ride on a very cold day at Talimena. To Kass Nichols for good food, a good place to keep my mule and a soft bed at Coyote Hills Ranch. To C.E. Tate for being crazy enough to ride with me when it was hot enough to fry and egg in your saddle seat and, also, for selling me his best mule. Last, but never least, thanks, to all the other riders Angela Bridge, Debbi Crew, Susan Friend, Kimberly Green, George Hamilton, Debbie Langley, Marjorie Lay, Mary Ben Marshall, Shane Richie, Sherry Robinson, Anita Thompson, Joe Wilson, Terri Wyatt, and Archie and Maxine Yeager. If there is any one I missed, thanks to you too, and please believe the oversight was unintentional.

This book is dedicated to Oklahoma Trail Riders....one and all.

Caution

Equestrian Unltd, Inc. and Betty Robinson assume no responsibility for the safety of any users of this trail guide. You alone are responsible for the decision to get on your horse and ride anywhere. Equestrian Unltd, Inc., the author and any land managers are in no way responsible for you getting lost, personal injury, animal injury, damage to property, or violation of laws in connection with the use of this book. Before starting out on any trail listed in this guide check with sponsoring agencies for current information regarding accessibility and condition of the trails.

Equestrian Unltd, Inc. and Betty Robinson are not responsible for erroneous or outdated information. If there is one thing that is consistent about trails, it is that they are constantly changing. Every effort was made at the time of research and at the time of printing to make all the details provided as accurate and current as possible. The trail maps in the book are meant as a guide. They are not drawn to scale.

Regarding directions, I have tried to be as specific as possible about how to get to trailheads. But roads change. Don't rely completely on my written directions. Pick up a state map or talk to locals to find if directions to the trails have changed. Nothing in this book implies the right to use private property. Trail rides on private property come and go at the whim of the owner. Always call before making plans and driving long distances. Every effort was made to include all the trails in Oklahoma so being listed is not an endorsement, but a statement to the fact the trail existed at the time of printing. All readers of this book are to use the information contained in it at their own risk.

Introduction

Thanks to my father, I have been riding horses since the age of three. During my childhood riding horses was synonymous with cowboys and Indians. I cut my teeth listening to Hank Tompson's song Oklahoma Hills, daydreaming of riding my pony across a reservation. It was a bitter disappointment to live in the wheat heart of north central Oklahoma where everything was fenced and cross fenced. I loved the wheat and farming but hated fences. I often asked Dad why he wasn't a rancher with hilly land and lots of wide open space. Of course, fences never limited my imagination nor did they slow down my riding. I'm still an avid horseperson and Oklahoma still brings to mind images of cowboys and Indians.

Indians have obviously had a profound and lasting impact on Oklahoma, from its name which literally translates 'Red People' to its state flag which features an Osage warrior's buckskin shield decorated with eagle feathers, crossed by an olive branch and peace pipe. Once the nation's largest Indian reservation, the tapestry of Oklahoma's history depicts the struggles of the Native Americans, the cowboys, the homesteader and the outlaw. Branded the "nations" because of the number of Native American tribes who were assigned lands and resettled there, Oklahoma became a formidable territory to travel across.

Long before the wild territory was ready for statehood, interested parties wrestled with each other for a toehold on the fertile plains. Cattlemen recognized the value of the rich grassland as they drove cattle north to trailheads in Kansas. East - west roads to the gold rushes in California and Colorado exposed the rich raw land to the restless land, hungry settler. After the cattlemen and settlers came, outlaws were attracted to this wild frontier because laws were hard to enforce. The landscape offered many places where outlaws and their gangs could hide. Indian territory became a safe haven for those wanted to evade the law.

The American people consummed by land hunger led the last great land rushes across Oklahoma. Her face was changed forever. Nothing can ever diminish the influence of the cowboy, or the Indian, but when the homesteader began to string barbed wire around their farms and across the plains the cattle drives stopped. Men wanted peace and security for their wives and children. More men were hired to enforce the law. In 1907, Oklahoma became the 47th state in the Union.

Today's travelers find Oklahoma a much easier place to cross. With I-35 running north and south and I-40 slicing the state east to west, most people don't have to experience more than the bumps on the Interstate unless they want to. People who stop to visit come in search of entertainment and recreation that still has the feel and flavor of the Old West and Oklahomans don't disappoint them.

More than 35 Native American tribes, including the Cherokee, Choctaw, Chickasaw, Creek, Seminole, Osage, Cheyenne, Sac and Fox, Delaware, Apache, and Pawnee just to name a few, share their culture and traditions through powwows and festivals. Cowboys show their skills and provide riding opportunities on working cattle ranches, dude ranches, and guest ranches. With over 203,528 registered quarter horses (not counting any other breed) in the state rodeos, horse racing, parades, horse shows and trail riding provide a variety of horse related entertainment.

Outdoor recreation plays a major role in the lives of Oklahomans, as well as, the visitors to the state. Each year trail riding increases in popularity as a way to enjoy the natural beauty of the state. This guide is designed with equine enthusiasts in mind, whether they are pleasure riders or the serious trial riders. The goal is to help locate and enjoy the many horse trails available for riding pleasure. Maps of each area indicate major roads and surrounding towns, as well as natural and historical points of interest unique to each trail.

Listings in this guide will help you choose the trails that suit you best, whether you prefer roughing it in a primitive camp or want the modern conveniences of a hot shower and electricity after a long ride.

The purpose of this book is not to tell you how to pack or camp with your horse. It is to provide information about individual trails. The guide will give you knowledge on how the trails are laid out, with distance and difficulty where available. Maps with primary land marks will be included for each trail if they were provided to the author.

The editor and the author take no responsibility for any one who gets lost using this guide. The author has made very effort to insure the accuracy of the information in this book at the time of printing HOWEVER, the one thing sure about trails is, they are ever changing. Use and vandalism take their toll. Trails sometimes exist at the whim of management. "Trail providers giveth and they taketh away". Ride all trails at your own risk. If you've never ridden the trail before pickup the most current map and information before starting out, most especially, if you are riding a Corp of Engineers maintained trail. The Corp trails generally follow lake flood plains and watersheds. The time of year can make a big difference in whether you find a dry or a boggy trail.

No matter which trails you choose, I know you will find something unique to enjoy. May all your trails end at camp.

About the Oklahoma Equestrian Trail Riders Association

by Ann Burnsed

The Oklahoma Equestrian Trail Riders Association is one of the biggest influences on the growth of trail riding in Oklahoma. Formed in 1974 for the purposes of promoting all types of trail riding and encouraging care of the horse, the organization was successful from the beginning. In 1990, membership grew to more than 350 families, which is sustained annually. Membership size makes OETRA one of the largest organizations of its kind in the nation. With members from eight states, this group has become more than just an Oklahoma organization.

In addition to sponsoring rides, OETRA is involved in related trail activities such as trail clinics and promoting the building and maintenance of state trails. OETRA was the first organization to participate in the State of Oklahoma's "Adopt-A-Trail" program by adopting the horse trails at Robbers Cave State Park. Members have maintained more than 40 miles of horse trail since 1982. State officials relied on OETRA members for guidance when they planned the Equestrian Campground at Robbers Cave, which opened in 1980. Members were also involved in planning the new horse camp at Cedar Lake.

The club has been instrumental in development of other horse trails and horse camping facilities though out the state. Donations from the club treasury are made regularly for developing and improving horse camping facilities and trails regardless of location in the state.

OETRA was one of the first to feature a mileage awards system. Created in 1975, horses and riders are recognized at mileage levels up to 3000 miles, with the 1000 mile award being a unique belt buckle designed especially for OETRA by Oklahoma artist Bob Bell of Okmulgee. The awards recognize pleasure riding as well as competitive and endurance riding.

In February 1991, OETRA received an award from the North American Trail Ride Conference for having sponsored 56 nationally sanctioned competitive rides, which was more than any other sponsor in the nation. The club now sponsors two competitive rides annually..."Indian Territory" at the John Zink Ranch near Tulsa, and "Robbers Route" at Robbers Cave State Park near Wilburton in southeast Oklahoma.

Probably the most valuable feature of the club is the monthly newsletter "The Trailrider" where updated listings of all pleasure, competitive and endurance rides are published regularly. No other publication is available with such complete coverage of ride dates, locations, and contacts, as well as local and regional news articles directed specifically to the trail riding public. An indispensable membership directory is also published annually.

Membership is open to anyone interested in promoting the purposes of the organization and riding Oklahoma's trails. Membership fee is $20 for a family or $15 for individuals (calendar year). Contact: Sylvia A. Rogers, Secretary, HC 32, Box 130, Lawton, OK 73501-9003.

Oklahoma Horse Trails

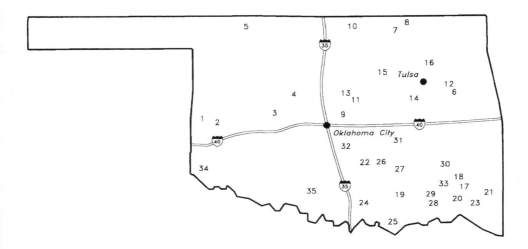

Reference List of Trails

Northwest Oklahoma
1. Black Kettle National Grasslands
2. Coyote Hills Ranch
3. Foss Lake Equestrian Trails
4. Roman Nose Horse Trails
5. Salt Plains Horse Trails

Northeast Oklahoma
6. Cherokee-Gruber WLMA
7. Camp Wah-Shah-She Horse Trails
8. Rocky Bluff Horse Trail
9. Bell Cow Horse Trails
10. Five Fingers Equestrian Trail
11. Horsethief Canyon
12. Jean Pierre Chouteau Trail
13. Lake Carl Blackwell Equestrian Trails
14. Okmulgee WLMA
15. Walnut Creek Equine Trails
16. Will Rogers Country Centennial Trail

Southeast Oklahoma
17. Billy Creek Trails
18. Cedar Lake Trails
19. Chickasaw National Recreation Horse Trail
20. Honobia Horse Trails
21. Horse Pen Trail
22. Indian Hills Ranch Horse Trails
23. Indian Mounds Horse Trails
24. Lake Murray Field Trial Trails
25. Platter-Lakeside Equestrian Trail
26. Lexington WLMA
27. Little River Boomtown Trails
28. McGee Creek Natural Scenic Recreation Horse Trails
29. McGee Creek WLMA
30. Robber's Cave Equestrian Trails
31. Sportsman Lake Horse Trails
32. Stanley Draper Lake Horse Trails
33. Talimena Horse Trails

Southwest Oklahoma
34. Sandy Sanders WLMA
35. Walker Creek Equestrian Trail

MAP LEGEND

Horse Trail		Interstate	
Interstate		U.S. Highway	
Paved Road		State Highways and Country Roads	
Gravel Road or Unimproved Dirt Road		Forest Roads	
Railroad		Pass, Bridge	
Cattle Guard		Hills	
Hiking Trail		River or Creek	
Point of Intrest		Waterfalls	
Well Pads		Lake or Pond	
Picnic Area		Wilderness Areas Boundary	
Building			
Campground		Recreation Areas National Monuments	
Public Parking			
Horse Camp			
Trailhead		Steep Trail	
Cave			
National, State Map Orientation		Trail Ride Location	

Horse Trails of Oklahoma

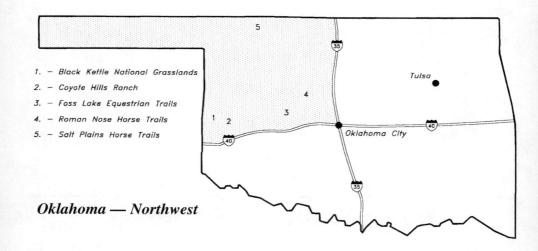

Oklahoma — Northwest

Black Kettle National Grasslands

Overview:

The Black Kettle National Grasslands are managed by the U.S. Department of Agriculture-Forest Service as part of the National Forest system. This system covers 31,301 acres near Cheyenne, Oklahoma and Canadian, Texas. They are managed to promote development of grasslands and for outdoor recreation, domestic livestock forage, water, and wildlife under the multiple-use principles.

These prairie lands were originally settled under Homestead laws. Farming was successful for a few years but poor farming practices combined with strong winds and prolonged drought encouraged what became known as the "great dust bowl". Families abandoned the worn-out farmsteads leaving the denuded land to the mercy of the rains. Water raced freely over the red earth gobbling up the last of the topsoil. With nothing to stop the rushing water giant gullies eroded the land. Local leaders turned to the Federal Government for help. Congress authorized the United States to purchase these lands under the Industrial Recovery Act of 1933. Soil Conservation Service began rehabilitation of the devastated lands. Grass, shrubs and trees were planted and grazing was restricted.

Much recovered, today these lands belong to you, the public. Even though the land is again grazed on a limited basis, recreation including horse back riding is encouraged. Hunters and fishermen take advantage of the abundant wildlife.

Location of the Riding Area:

To get to the National Grasslands near Cheyenne, OK take exit 20 of I-40 at Sayre, follow U.S. 283 north 28 miles to Cheyenne, then take S. H. 47 west to a sign that indicates Battle of the Washita. The office is right near the corner on the right. Pick up maps and instructions here.

Camp Facilities Summary:

Type: day use
Fees: None
Electric: None

Rest rooms: None
Showers: None
Water: None; in the dry season you may not find any for your horses.

Trail Summary:

Type: Public; day use
Terrain: Grass land pasture; low hills; red deep, steep gullies; some trees.
Difficulty: easy to moderate
Length: Choose your own. There are no marked trails. Set your own time.
Trail Markers: None

Trail Notes:

Most, if not all, the Black Kettle Grassland is open for horse back riding. You won't find marked trails but you won't be riding in deep valleys or mountain sides covered in trees either, so getting lost should not be that big of a problem. The hills are bright red and stubby compared to Arkansas and eastern Oklahoma, but they have an magnetism all their own. The Black Kettle Grassland is a checker board pattern which might create a problem for those trail riders used to riding several hours at one time. However, the country is beautiful and the land intriguing.

The ranger who oversees the area indicated that some of the land is fenced because it was collected by the government from tax delinquent farms. When you ride in the area if a gate is open leave it that way. If the gate is closed be sure to shut it. If you choose to ride in the grassland be sure when you ask for direction to best area for riding, also ask for specific information on where you can park your trailer. That was the part I found the hardest. I could find areas marked as grassland but I often couldn't find any place for my trailer.

Because this is a day use area you might want to check with Coyote Hills Ranch as a place to say overnight. **See listing under Guest Ranches**.

The ranger recommended Unit 66 for starters. For $3.00 you may purchase a map of the area. The office is open Monday through Friday 8 to 4:30.

Nearest Services:

Several small towns are scattered around near the grasslands. Because the grassland covers such a wide area you will need to consult an Oklahoma map for the town nearest to the area where you plan to ride.

For More Information:

The District Ranger's Office
Black Kettle National Grasslands
P.O. Box 266
Cheyenne, OK 73628
405-497-2143

Horse Sense and Safety

- Try out new equipment at home. If something is going to rub, gall, or get loose and fall off, let it happen while you are close to help.
- Before you leave your vehicle be sure you are not blocking a road or driveway. See if you have left room for others to park and unload safely.
- If your horse paws the ground, do not tie to trees. Tie to your own trailer, use tree savers or teach your horse to hobble. Pawing not only damages the ground and trees, it damages your horses hooves.
- Be aware of the physical capabilities of your horse, yourself, and those riding with you.
- If you don't have a trail bridle, leave your halter on under your bridle or pack it with you so you won't be tempted to tie by the bridle reins. More horses get loose, break bridles or reins, and hurt themselves or someone else because they are carelessly tied.
- When riding in the woods, if you must tie to a tree, be sure the tree you choose is alive and sturdy. Don't choose one that is dead and can easily be pulled over by the horse. This can cause a real run away.
- When you hang your haynet to the picket poll or trailer, be sure to tie it high enough the horse can't get his foot in it.
- Thunderstorms and their lightning are just as dangerous at the edges as in the middle. Move quickly at the first sign of such a storm. Never take refuge under a single tree. Find a group of trees and go as deep in the grove as you can. Get yourself and your horse as low to the ground as possible. The safest place for you and your horse during a lightning storm is in your horse trailer.
- Do your part in keeping the trailhead clean and accessible to others. On streets and paved parking lots, pick up your animal's manure. In dirt lots scatter it.

Coyote Hills Ranch

Overview:

The town of Cheyenne is located in Rogers Mills county in far western Oklahoma. History is more than plentiful tracing back to General Custer and the Battle of the Washita. The land is robust, red rolling hills and pasture land. Coyote Hills Ranch will help, from one to many, enjoy the flavor of the old west.

Location of Trail:

Coyote Hills ranch sits midway between Oklahoma City, OK and Amarillo, TX and is close to I-40. Take exit 20 off I-40 at Sayre, and follow U.S. 283 north 28 miles to Cheyenne, then take S.H. 47 west four miles. At this intersection you will see a ranch sign. Turn right or north for two miles and west until you drive into the ranch. Call for reservations.

Camp Summary:

Type: Private
Fees: Yes, call for information.
Electric: Yes

Restrooms: Yes, flush toilets
Showers: yes, hot water
Water: yes, both people and horses

Trail Summary:

Type: Private
Terrain: rolling red hills and grassland pasture
Difficulty: easy
Length: varies according to riders choice and ability

Trail Notes:

Trails on the Coyotes Hills Ranch wind over hills and pastures. The amount of riding on the actual ranch is limited but there are roads to ride and the ranch is also close to the Black Kettle National Grassland. See other listing. (Guest Ranch & Black Kettle Grassland)

Rules and Responsibilities:

Check at the office.

Nearest Services:

The nearest camping supplies, gas, groceries and restaurants can be found in Cheyenne. Major services such as hospitals and vet can be found in Sayre.

For Information Contact:

Coyote Hills Ranch, Inc.
P.O. Box 99
Cheyenne, OK 73628
405-497-2143

Foss Lake Equestrian Trails

Overview:

The high prairie that surrounds Foss Lake was formerly part of the Cheyenne-Arapaho Indian reservation. Most of the land was settle during the famous land run of 1892. The land has been through booms, the dust bowl and depression, yet it still looks much the same today as it did years ago. Foss Lake was created by construction of the world's largest earth dam, 134 feet high and 3 miles long. This dam blocks the Washita River and provides 8800 acres of water for recreation. Equestrian trails have been established along the shore.

Location of Trail:

Between Clinton and Elk City, OK exit I-40 at number 53. Proceed 7 miles on Hwy 44. At the intersection of 44 & 73 highways you will see a gift shop on the right. This is also the park office. Stop here for current information. To get to the equestrian camp follow Hwy 73 to Mouse Creek campground. The entrance is on the right. As you pull into this area stay to your right. You will find a short loop that circles a locust grove. On the backside of the loop you will find the horse camp with picket poles and all the extras.

Camp Summary:

Type: Public; day use or overnight camping.
Fees: Yes, call for information.
Electric: Yes
Restrooms: Yes, flush toilets
Showers: Yes, hot water
Water: Yes, both people and horse

Trail Summary:

Type: Public trails
Terrain: Trails parallel the lake shore. Some rolling hills, pasture and woods.
Difficulty: Easy
Length: About 14 miles

Trail Markers: Mostly mowed with a brush hog at the time of printing. Permanent markers were to be added.

Maps: Not available at time of printing.

Trail Notes:

Trails were basically still under construction when I rode there. It was flat grassland with good views of the lake. Cottonwood, locust and elm were the main trees. Some road riding some pasture riding. Almost all of it parallels the lake. Check with the office for the latest information.

Rules and Responsibilities:

Check at the Office.

Nearest Services:

The nearest camping supplies, gas, groceries and restaurants can be found at convenience stores along the lake front. Major services such as hospitals and vet can be found in Clinton or Elk City.

For Information Contact:

Foss State Park
HC66 Box 11
Foss, OK 73647-9622
405-592-4433

Roman Nose Horse Trails

Overview:

Like all the exciting horse trail areas in Oklahoma, Watonga's history is interwoven with the life and times of prominent Native Americans. The town was founded in 1892 when the Cheyenne-Arapaho reservation was open to settlement. The town is named for the Arapaho chief, Watonga. Cheyenne Chief Henry Roman Nose, for whom the park area was named took part of the park land as his allotment. He lived there until his death in 1917. His dugout was at the Spring of Everlasting Waters.

Location of the Trail:

Take Hwy 8 north out of Watonga to 8A. Follow 8A into the park. As you enter the park you will see the lodge and office to your right. Be careful not to pull down in there; there is not much room to turn big trailers around.
Continue on 8A. You will come to a large "Y" in the road. Right in front of you is the Roman Nose Stable. If you are planning to rent and ride, you

have arrived. If you are pulling your own horse follow the left fork of the "Y" about 75 yards. Don't go into group camping. Take the next right when you see the red pipe corrals. There are pull-throughs and back-ins for equestrians. Once you have chosen your corral or saddled up, go to the stable office and check in. You must show your Coggins papers and pay fees.

Camp Facilities Summary:

Type: Day use or overnight camping
    There are five camping sites which may be reserved by calling the stable.
        Pens (16 X 16) are on a first come first serve basis.
Fees: Day use is $3.00 per day per horse to ride. $6.00 a night to camp.
Electric: None
Restroom: None
Showers: None
Water: Yes for both people and horses. There is a community tank but there is also water to fill your personal buckets.

Trail Summary:

Type: Public use with minimum day use fee.
Terrain: Up and down hills, through the junipers, across chocky white rock and through some gypsum rock formations.
Difficulty: Easy.
Length: Because these trails started for the stable horses the ride is more for time than mileage.
    If you are looking for miles this is not the trail to choose.
Trail Markers: I'm not sure there are any trail markers. These trails wind around a great deal very near the stable most of the time you just sort of know where you are going.
Trail Maps: There are no trail maps per se. However, there is a flyer prepared by Oklahoma Parks & Resorts called Roman Nose Resort Park Stables. This gives you an overall view of what is available and where you can ride.

Trail Notes:

The camping spot for Roman Nose is very nice. Along with a lot of shade each campsite has a picnic table and grill. Calling ahead will assure a site when you arrive. The corrals are a plus for riders that want to spend the night or the weekend with their horse. Water is handy. A small stream runs by which adds some atmosphere. The biggest problem I see is that unless you know someone who lives in the area and has access to more riding space you are pretty land locked here. I can highly recommend seeing the place. It is very unique. But if you are a long distance rider you will feel limited. This spot is great for someone from a larger suburban area that needs a place to get out even for a short distance with their horse. Or for someone like me that is traveling and wants a safe place to rest up. This is a great place to let your horse rest and you can also give them some minimum exercise.

Rental Policies:

Roman Nose Stables offers one, two or three-hour trail rides over picturesque canyon country. Each trail ride group is accompanied by a guide dressed as an authentic 19th century personality. The guide will provide tales of lost treasure, outlaws, cowboys, cavalry and the heritage of the Native American.

All trail rides are $10.00 an hour and advanced reservations of horses can be made for most dates. A three hour dinner ride is $40.00 per person.

Riding Rules and Responsibilities:

Horse traffic is prohibited on Lake Watonga Dam or spillways.

Horse traffic is prohibited in any camp areas other than the equestrian camp and it's adjoining overflow area below the stable.

Horse traffic is prohibited on road beds except (1) from "Pack Saddle" and bottom area to trail entry by the stable, (2) from north end of riding area behind stable to Lake Boecher Dam so that the east riding area can be accessed.

Be courteous and safe with hikers and bicyclists.

Stay within designated riding areas.

Nearest Services:

Food and lodging can be found in the park. For gas, feed, veterinary, or personal health needs Watonga is the nearest town.

For More Information:

Roman Nose Resort
Box 61
Watonga, OK, 73772
405-623-7281

Salt Plains Horse Trails

Overview:

The Salt Plains are a perfectly flat expanse of mud and salt completely devoid of vegetation, located in north central Oklahoma. These flats are awesome in their desolation. Seven miles long and three miles wide this strip of white salt and mud flats is what gives Salt Plains its name. This is the only spot in the world where people can dig for the "hourglass" selenite crystals. In addition to the salt flats and crystal digging there is much more to see and do. A national wildlife refuge borders the park and more than 250 species of birds migrate through these crossroads. Some of the most interesting species include the eagle, sandhill crane, and pelican. Now equestrians can also enjoy the area. New trails and a horse camp are in the plans for fall of 1997.

Location of the Trail:

From the junction of U.S. Hwy 11 and State Hwy 38, follow 38 south to the Corp of Engineers office. This office is just across the dam on the right. At the office ask for directions to parking and where the most area for riding is located.

Camp Facilities Summary:

There are no specific facilities at the time of printing but facilities should be available by fall 1997.

Trail Summary:

Type: Public; equestrian
Terrain: Flat mostly pasture land. Lake boundary.
Difficulty: Easy
Length: Unknown at this time

Trail Notes:

The Ranger at Salt Plains has favored horse trails for the last three years. If riders in the area would show support it could happen soon. There are plans for trails and camping on the north side of the river. I used Salt Plains as a stopover with my mules when on a trip to Kansas. I found it a great place to rest up. The people are friendly and make you feel welcome.

Rules and Regulations:

Check with the local ranger.

Nearest Services:

Services for picnic supplies and groceries can be found at the convenience stores near the lake. For major services such as veterinary or hospital, Cherokee or Alva would be the closest.

For More Information:

Great Salt Plains State Park
Rt. 1, Box 28,
Jet, OK 73749
405-626-4731

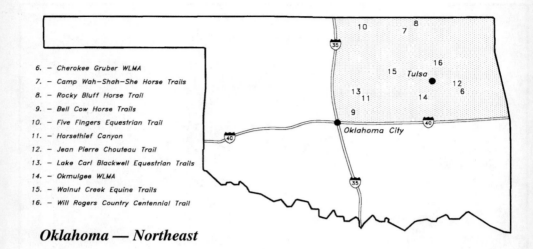

6. – Cherokee Gruber WLMA
7. – Camp Wah-Shah-She Horse Trails
8. – Rocky Bluff Horse Trail
9. – Bell Cow Horse Trails
10. – Five Fingers Equestrian Trail
11. – Horsethief Canyon
12. – Jean Pierre Chouteau Trail
13. – Lake Carl Blackwell Equestrian Trails
14. – Okmulgee WLMA
15. – Walnut Creek Equine Trails
16. – Will Rogers Country Centennial Trail

Oklahoma — Northeast

Cherokee Gruber Wildlife Management Area

Overview:

The Cherokee Gruber Wildlife Management Area has a long military history. For years Camp Gruber has been used for military training and exercises. When you ride or picnic on Little Round Mountain you can still find pieces of shrapnel from artillery practice. Part of the land is now used for public hunting under the management of the Oklahoma Department of Wildlife.

Location of the Trail:

The trail head is located east of Muskogee. From the Muskogee Turnpike take Hwy 62 east to Midway Gas Station approximately 13 miles. You will see a sign announcing Cherokee Gruber Public Hunting Area. Turn south and continue about a mile and a half. As you approach the area the road will curve around a mountain. Presently the blacktop will continue left and there will be a gravel road directly in front of you, take this to the camp area.

Camp Facilities Summary:

Type: Public. May NOT be used by equestrians between September 15 and January 1.
Fees: None
Electric: None
Restroom: Primitive toilets
Showers: None
Water: For animals only

Trail Summary:

Type: Public; overnight and day use
Terrain: Open pasture, some trees, woods, and some rocks but not too bad.
Difficulty: Easy.
Length: Most of the trails are unmarked. There is 22,000 acres. Set your own mileage.
Trail Markers: Some markers on trees.
Trail Maps: None

Trail Notes:

Although you can unload to ride as soon as you enter the Cherokee Gruber management area the best camping spot is four miles down the gravel road. The campground is pretty obvious once you pass the two primitive toilets. There is lots of shade, plenty of elbow room, and a clear flowing stream nearby that you can water from.

Because this area is made up of 22,000 acres there is a lot of trail to ride without riding the same trail several times. Personally, I like to ride this kind of trail. People who want to road ride will find enough of that to keep them happy but, there is miles of single track trail through the woods, open meadow, and along Green Leaf Creek. You can ride over to Round Mountain for lunch. That is the mountain that used to be used for artillery practice. It is an interesting place to visit. Of course wildlife is abundant in this area. If you ride quiet and ride early or at dusk you have a good chance to see lots of deer, as well as raccoon, bobcat, and squirrel.

There are some problems with the area. For one the trails are not marked except for one. Most of the people learn the area by riding the roads and then learn the wooded trails in between. A second problem is that the area is closed to riding 3 ½ months out of the year from September to January. BUT, the most critical problem is ticks. The ticks here are plentiful, abundant, profuse, whatever word you want to use to say too-darn-many. These ticks also don't pay much attention to any kinds of repellant. The best time to ride in this area is before or after tick season when it is cold. Otherwise come prepared to pick them off both you and your animals.

Trail Rules and Responsibilities:

All rules for riding in WLMA apply

Nearest Services:

All services can be found in Muskogee or Tahlequah. Ice and picnic supplies can be found at the midway service station where you turned of Hwy 62.

For More Information:

Oklahoma Department of Wildlife Conservation
P.O. Box 53465
Oklahoma City OK 73105
405-521-2739

Camp Wah-Shah-She Horse Trail

Overview:

The land surrounding Wah-Shah-She Trail is saturated with history of the Osage Nation. The first settler in the area set up a trading post on the Caney River where trade was established between the Osage and Chouteau's American Fur Trading Company in 1860. The nearby town of Barnsdall was originally called Bigheart named after Chief Jim Bigheart of the Osage Nation. The Midland Valley Railroad pushed the first tracks into the Osage Reservation and built a station at Bigheart in 1905.

Camp Wah-Shah-She is 524 acres nestled in the wooded hills of Osage County. By tradition it is a Girl Scout camp, however, many other groups hold meetings and conferences in the quiet atmosphere. Local equestrians use the numerous trails that loop around the main compound.

Location of the Trail:

Wah-Shah-She Horse Trail is located at Wah-Shah-She Girl Scout Camp. From Bartlesville take Hwy 123 approximately 8 1\2 miles to a camp sign, take a black top to the right to a stone house and turn right again. Follow this black top to a mail box that says Wah-Shah-She and turn left. As you enter the camp you will cross two cattle guards. One out by the road and the other near the Ranger's house. There is parking near the Ranger's house and just past the A-Ki-Ki-Pa sign on the left. You may also ask the Ranger for other suggestions.

Camp Facilities Summary:

Type: Day use
Fees: None
Electric: None
Restroom: None
Showers: None
Water: None

Trail Summary:

Type: Day use with permission.

Terrain: Open pasture, some trees, woods, and rocks.
Difficulty: Easy.
Length: Choose your length, the trail is organized into short loops.
Trail markers: None
Trail Maps: Yes

Trail Notes:

This trail is laid out in loops around areas used by Girls Scouts. Most of the time there is no one there and you are free to ride any where you want. When camp is in session you must ask permission and frequently can not use the facilities while the campers are present.

The riding is easy. It is mostly pasture or grassland with some tree cover.

Camp Rules and Responsibilities:

Do not tie horses to trees.
Be sure to stay on the trail
No loose or hobbled horses

Nearest Services:

All services are in Bartlesville, Oklahoma about 10 miles.

For More Information:

Bluestem Girl Scout Council
511 E. 11th Street
Bartlesville, Oklahoma 74003
918-336-3378

Rocky Bluff Horse Trail

Overview:

Copan traces its roots to a trading post that served the Delawares, Osages, and Cherokees in the area. In those years few people in the wide open ranch land made it hard for small communities to grow. The construction of Copan Dam was an economic boon to the area.

Location of the Trail:

Rocky Buff Horse trail is located just east of the dam and project office on Hwy 10 near Copan, OK. The trail head is marked by yellow and black horse crossing signs.

Camp Facilities Summary:

Type: Day use
Fees: None
Electric: None
Restroom: None
Showers: None
Water: None

Trail Summary:

Type: Public, day use
Terrain: Open pasture, some trees, woods, and rocks. Most of the trail parallels the lake shore.
Difficulty: Easy
Length: Four miles with plans for some additions
Trail markers: Unknown
Trail Maps: None

Trail Notes:

The trail is four miles in length with a gravel parking area on each end. The terrain varies from flat upland prairie grass to more rugged timber cov-

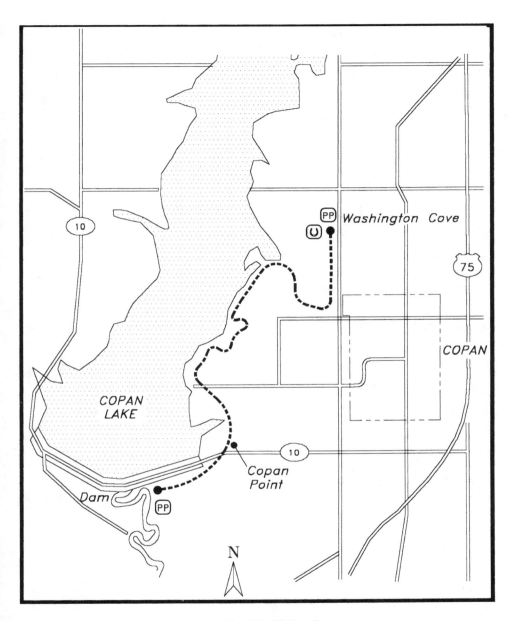

Rocky Bluff Trail

ered areas. Only horses and pedestrians are allowed on the trail. The trail winds through archery-only Corps managed property. No firearms are allowed. The trails is open all year round. Maintained by local volunteers.

Camp Rules and Responsibilities:

Do not tie horses to trees.
Be sure to stay on the trail
No loose or hobbled horses

Nearest Services:

Gas, Groceries, and picnic supplies in Copan. Feed, veterinary services and health care in Dewey or Bartlesville.

For More Information:

Lake Manager
Corp. Of Engineers,
Copan Lake Office
Route 1, Box 260
Copan, OK 74022-9762

Bell Cow Horse Trails

Overview:

Chandler is a quiet community with a small town atmosphere. In the early morning a local rooster crows loud enough you can hear him when you drive down Main Street. In the 1800s Chandler had great promise of becoming a large industrial center, but a major tornado in 1887did so much damage the town never fully recovered. Although the commerical dreams of the early town leaders never came into being, the county did prosper in the number of horse thieves. William Tilghman, premier lawman from Dodge City, Kansas was elected sheriff of Lincoln county and during his first thirty days he was handed nine warrants, each for the arrest of a horse thief. He arrested eight of the desperados and recovered the horse in the ninth case. In more recent history Old Route 66 adds its charm. Chandler is a must see town built around the old time square with lots of interesting small stores that beg you to stop and shop.

Location of the Trail:

Follow Hwy. 18 north out of Chandler and cross over the Turner Turnpike. A green and white sign directs you left on a blacktop road. You will come to a wide swinging curve. Don't follow the curve to your right unless you want to go to the headquarters first. Straight ahead on the gravel road takes you to horse camp.

Camp Facilities Summary:

Type: Public, day use or overnight camping
Fees: Day use is $2.00 per day per horse. $5.00 a night to camp.
Electric: Yes
Restroom: Yes, flush toilets
Showers: Yes, hot water
Water: Yes for both people and horses.

Trail Summary:

Type: Public, with minimum day use fee.
Terrain: Open pasture, some trees, woods, and rocks. Most of the trail parallels the lake shore.
Difficulty: Easy.
Length: There are two sections of trails, each is an out and back. Flat Rock Trail is 5.9 miles. Red Bud trail is 12.7. **You can not ride all the way around the lake,** some of the area is just too boggy. People have tried to make the loop but couldn't make it and had to be hauled back into camp. So because this is an out and back trail be sure to double your mileage to figure riding time.
Trail Markers: Trails are marked with paint on trees and ribbons. Be sure to look everywhere for the markers. The location of the markers vary with what is available to put them on.
Trail Maps: Yes, check with lake headquarters.

Trail Notes:

The camp is big, open and well maintained. There is room for even the largest trailers. Camp sites include nice large picket polls with some shade. For those who don't want to ride there is a place to swim and fish.

Flat Rock Trail goes west. The Red Bud Trail goes east. The trails are

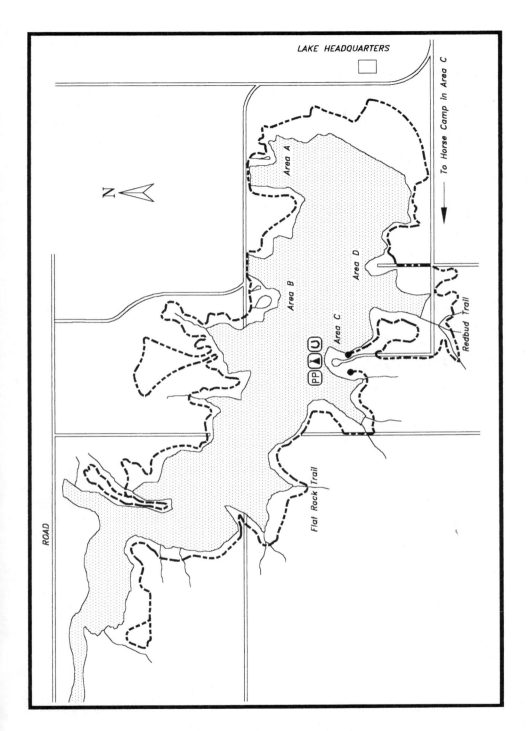

Bell Cow Lake Horse Trails

single track most of the way marked with orange blazes on trees. On the Red Bud Trail you begin by circling down through some slab rock near the lake. As you come out of this sections you will be facing a fence. Cross the road, go through a gate, and continue near the blacktop for about a quarter of mile. Some of the trees along this stretch are marked with paint to let you know you are in the right place. The trail is well cared for and maintained Lost Creek has a neat crossing that shows the creativity and effort of the trail builders.

At point B, after rounding one end of the lake, you will find more restrooms, and a place to picnic.

This set of trails is located between Oklahoma City and Tulsa just off the Turner Turnpike. This is not only a great place for a day ride, but it is also a good stopover for long distance travelers. Hot showers and room to exercise and rest the horses.

Camp Rules and Responsibilities:

Do not tie horses to trees.
Be sure to stay on the trail
Bag manure and old hay and take it home with you (They are trying to change this. It is best to check the regulations when you arrive.)
No loose or hobbled horses

Nearest Services:

Gas, groceries, feed or veterinary care can be found as close as Chandler.

For More Information:

Bell Cow Lake Headquarters
1001 S. Steele
Chandler, OK 74834
405-258-3212
405-258-1460

Five Fingers Equestrian Trail

Overview:

Five Fingers Equestrian Trail lies east of Ponca City, Oklahoma in the edge of the Osage oil boom area. It is near the community of Burbank. In 1902 the Eastern Oklahoma Railway ran across the western edge of the Osage nation. Near the right-of-way along Salt Creek cockleburs grew thick on a rocky bluff. Railroad men called this the burr bank. When a post office was established in 1907, it was named Burbank. You will still see a few cockleburs a long the trail when you ride from Burbank Landing to Sarge Creek.

Many of the small towns in the area had their origins tied to the oil boom. Most of them are now ghost towns. Old Kaw City became a ghost town for fish, when it was swallowed by the man-made lake which carries its name.

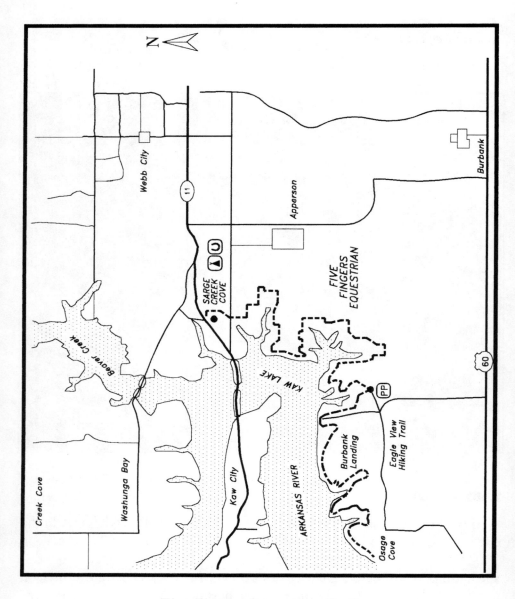

Five Fingers Equestrian Trail

Location of the Trail:

Burbank Landing is located about 3 miles north of U.S. Hwy 60 between Ponca City and Pawhuska, Oklahoma. The road to the landing is gravel and very dusty in the summer time. As you approach the parking area the road will "T". Turn right, you are in the parking lot.

Sarge Cove is located approximately 2.8 miles east of Kaw City on Hwy. 11. When you turn off the highway, take the next left turn and continue to the first group of trees, the parking lot near the amphitheatre is for day use.

Camp Facilities Summary:

Type: Day use and overnight camping. For overnight camping use Sarge Creek. No overnight camping at Burbank Landing.
Fee: Yes, there is a minimal fee for overnight camping.
Electric: Yes, 10 sites
Restrooms: Yes
Showers: Yes
Water: Yes, for both people and horses

Trail Summary:

Type: Public; day use
Terrain: Open pasture, some trees, woods, and a few rocks. Most of the trail parallels the lake shore.
Difficulty: Easy
Length: From Burbank Landing to Sarge Cove is 16.3 miles. From Burbank Landing to Osage Cove is 11 miles. The eleven mile trail is a multi-use trail. As long as hikers do not object equestrans may use it.
Trail Markers: Ribbons and Karsonite markers.
Trail Maps: No specific maps at this time except for this book.

Trail Notes:

The trailhead at Burbank begins at the north side of the parking lot or to your left if you are facing the barrier that has been put in to divide the parking lot. Ride over that bank and the trail begins almost immediately.

Because the trail is 16.3 miles long, riders most often ride out eight or nine miles from either end and then turn around to ride back. Riders who move their trailers from one end to the other and ride the whole distance sometimes find the middle stretch a little grown up. The trail runs parallel to the shoreline from Burbank Landing to Sarge Creek Cove. Because the trail is not actually down on the shoreline you don't have to worry about riding into bogs. The only place you have to look for a bog is when you cross the "Big Gully". Coming from Sarge Creek the spot is marked with a Karsonite marker and the words, Caution Boggy. If you are riding in the rainy season or if you are riding with a large number of riders, it pays to be careful here.

Often the trail is single track winding through cool shaded woods. Other times you break out of the tree cover and have a magnificent view of the lake and dam. Bird watchers will love this trail; the variety of birds is phenomenal. In the winter time eagles are often seen fishing along the shore line.

You must check with the Corps of Engineers and make reservations for overnight camping. There are 10 electrical hookups, water, covered shelter, and a large area for tent camping. There are no facilities for keeping horses. The Corp recommends portable corrals, tying to trailers, or picketing.

Nearest Services:

Hospital, veterinary, gas, food, and feed are in Ponca City. Camping supplies can be found at convenience stores near the lake.

For more information:

Corps of Engineers
RR 2, Box 500
Ponca City, OK 74604-9629
405-762-5611

Horsethief Canyon

Overview:

Horsethief Canyon is one of Oklahoma's most interesting historical sites. Indian artifacts left behind tell of the canyon use since the era of the big game hunters 5,000 B.C. In the early 1700's explorer Washington Irving recounted his travels through the area. Later the Canyon became part of the Creek nation but when the tribe was relocated the land was given to the Iowa reservation.

The famous Chisolm Cattle Trail is located 5 miles west. The roving cattle grazed where they would up and down the valley. The area to the north and west of the canyon was coveted grassland and became known as Cowboy Flats. Because the Canyon remained part of the Iowa reservation even after "the run of 1889" that opened so much of Indian Territory to white settlement, outlaws stayed there out of reach of the law. It was easy to cross into cattle country pick up some livestock and hide them in the canyon. Today you may take your own horse to the Canyon and ride the same trails. Call for information.

Location of Trail:

The canyon and trails are located 9 miles south of Stillwater, OK. Go through Perkins on Hwy 177 and cross the Cimarron River. Immediately turn west and follow the main road for 8 miles to the Horsethief Camp compound.

Camp Summary:

Type: Day use or overnight camping on weekends.
Fees: Camping fees may change from year to year. Call for information.
Electric: None
Restrooms: Yes, primitive toilets
Showers: None
Water: Yes, both people and horses

Trail Summary:

Type: Private campground. There is a charge for camping and riding the trails. Call for current charges.

Terrain: Red hills and pastures. Few rocks, some trees.
Difficulty: Easy
Length: Determined by the individual
Trail Markers: None
Maps: None

Trail Notes:

The trails are along the river bank and across rolling pastures. Most of the rides are led by Ben Holder. For people with their own horses he often leads them a short ways until they become comfortable with the trails and then he puts them on their own. Always watch for bogs around ponds when looking for water and along the river during the rainy season.

Rules and Responsibilities:

Do not tie horses directly to trees.
If gates are open leave them open. If they are shut be sure to shut them.
Check with Ben or Teresa for any further rules.

Nearest Services:

The nearest camping supplies, gas, groceries and restaurants can be found in Perkins. Major services such as hospital and veterinary can be found in Stillwater.

For Information Contact:

Horsethief Canyon
P.O. Box 772
Perkins, OK 74059
405-547-2262

Jean Pierre Chouteau Trail

Overview:

The Verdigris River, which meanders beside the Chouteau Trail, holds a romantic and colorful role in the history of Oklahoma. The Three Forks area, just below the Chouteau Lock and Dam, is the confluence of the Grand (Neosho), the Verdigris and the Arkansas River. For many years the Three Forks area was the center of exchange for products of the trappers, Indian,

French and other western wanderers. The continuous mobility of vicinity population caused local mission schools to flourish and then decline. The Indians who occupied this area included the Osages, Cherokees and Creeks. During the Civil War, this area was the scene of bitter guerrilla fighting between the Northern and Southern factions of the nation.

The Chouteau Lock is named for Col. Auguste P. Chouteau, son of Jean Pierre Chouteau, who established the first permanent white settlement in Oklahoma at the present site of Salina in 1796. He built a complete shipyard on the banks of the river and brought Creole carpenters from New Orleans and St. Louis to construct keelboats in which the traders shipped their furs and produce down the Arkansas and ultimately down the Mississippi to New Orleans.

In April, 1824, General Matthew Arbuckle brought 121 officers and enlisted men to set up Cantonment Gibson, (Fort Gibson).

> *"Enlisted men received five dollars a month, ate salt pork and beans, and performed monotonous duties. Hard labor, heat, flies, mosquitoes, malaria, fever, and bad liquor took their toll. During the first eleven and a half years 507 men died, earning the fort the label "Graveyard of the West."* (Fugate, 1991).

Representative of all the major wars in which the United States has participated are buried in the National Cemetery located one mile from the town of Ft. Gibson - the earliest dates begin in 1824. Washington Irving visited here in 1832 and Sam Houston lived in the area from 1829 to 1832.

The early settlement was known by several names: Falls City, Verdigris Falls, Verdigris Landing, Three Forks, Creek Agency and Sleepyville. When the railroad came in 1871, the town moved north to the present site of Okay. This little town was also known by several names Coretta Switch, North Muskogee, Rex and finally Okay.

The Inola and Tiawah area near the second lock and dam is a quiet community with a number of Mennonite farmers whose wagons and buggies can still be seen on the roadways. This county like several other in Oklahoma was the stomping grounds of Belle Starr. Her son, James Edward Reed, is buried in Tiawah.

---

* Historical information in this section was provided by US Army Corps of Engineers material and by Fugate's Roadside Guide to Oklahoma.

Location of the Trail:

The Jean Pierre Chouteau Trail is located alongside the McClellan-Kerr Arkansas River Navigational System from a point near Tulsa's Port of Catoosa to Fort Gibson, Oklahoma. Although this trail was originally designed for hiking, portions of it have been redesigned for equestrian use. At the time of this writing, two sections are recommended for riders. One is from Rocky Point to Afton Landing, the other is from Chouteau Lock & Dam to Fort Gibson. You may reach the Rocky Point or the Newt Graham trail access from SH 33 or 412 west of Chouteau. Signs mark significant turns. Newt Graham is about seven miles down a black top road. No over night camping facilities. There is no camping here without permission. Day use only.

Afton Landing is located off SH 51 west of Wagoner. A portion of Afton Landing has been unofficially set aside for horsemen; however you still need to get permission from the Corps office if you plan to stay overnight. **Be aware literature states the trail must cross HWY 51 bridge to or from the Afton camp ground.** This is a busy highway.

The last section of the horse trail travels to or from Chouteau Lock # 17 Visitors center to Fort Gibson. This is the trickiest part of the trail because of a number of water crossings which have to be avoided. This also means avoiding private property in some places. Access the lock from SH 251A out of Okay. You must be on the east side of the river channel to access the trail. The hikers may cross the lock with permission but horses may not. Therefore you must trailer to the east side or ride from Fort Gibson out and back.

Fort Gibson Trailhead is located just across the river from the Old Fort Stockade. From the Stockade turn left over the railroad tracks proceed across the bridge and turn left again.

Camp Facilities Summary:

Type: Public
Fees: None
Electric: None
Showers: None
Water: None

Trail Summary:

Type: Public use; no fees

Terrain: Flat, most of it parallels the Arkansas River Navigational system. A few trees, but mostly open. Water crossings can be tricky. Cross with care.
Difficulty: Moderate because of some of the water crossings.
Length: Rocky Point to Afton, 18.5 miles.
      Chouteau Lock and Dam to Fort Gibson, 11.5 miles
Trail Markers: Karsonite or wooden posts at trailheads. Be aware the markers are not always there. In most places the trail is pretty straight forward because it follows the river navigation channel.

Trail Notes:

Camp facilities for horses or mules users are limited. Even though two sections of this trail are open to horses, they still appear to be an after thought. At the time I rode this trail it had been extremely neglected. Camp facilities were badly vandalized. Locals do not consider some camps to be safe after dark. The best way to ride this trail because it is a continuous trail with no loops, is to leap frog trailers or ride out and back for a day ride. If you plan to stay out overnight travel in a group. Plan on carrying your own people and horse water unless you check in advance with the Corps office. Even though you are close to water most of the time, there are few easy places to get your animal to it.

While this trail is sixty miles in length, the two segments which are open to trail riders are much more limited. The portion from Rocky Point to Afton landing is 18.5 miles. From Chouteau Lock and Dam to Fort Gibson Park is 11.5 miles. This is a total of thirty miles but it can not be ridden straight through. There is no horse trail between Afton Landing and Lock # 17.

Except for Rocky Point and Newt Graham the hardest part about riding this trail is finding the actual access to the trail. The two locations just mentioned are easy. You can see the trail markers from where you unload. However, at Afton Landing you have to cross the bridge and the highway to Guthrie Cotton Port of Dunkin. The trail begins behind the park. At the Fort Gibson park you have to ride two or three miles of road to get to the actual trail.

Because of limited time and heat, I rode the sections of trail near Newt Graham lock. The trail was dry at that time. It was well mowed and easy to stay on. The saddling area was probably the biggest disappointment. Absolutely no shade or water. You had to saddle in a concrete parking lot.

The trail crosses flat, open grassland which offers excellent views of the navigation channel. It winds through densely wooded bottomlands where oak, hickory, sycamore, and pecan trees are plentiful. The trail has a lot of potential for people who don't mind the out and back rides or for those who have help in leap frogging their trailers.

Special consideration: Before bringing horses or mules on Corps-managed land remember the following:
- Horses are prohibited in developed campgrounds and public use areas. Primitive camping privileges are available for horse riders at equestrian trails.
- Horses may not be hobbled or turned loose to graze. You must bring all feed and hay with you.
- Tie horses to the trailer or picket line at night. Picket lines should be knotted to prevent horses from reaching the trees at either end and chewing the bark. Horses should not be tied directly to a tree overnight. If it is absolutely necessary to tie a horse to a tree while on the trail, care should be taken to avoid tree damage by preventing bark chewing.
- Use caution when watering horses on the trail. Check the shoreline for soft boggy ground before riding or leading your mount down to drink. This is especially important during dry weather, when the lake elevation may be below normal.
- Several trails traverse agricultural or grazing leases and have gates across them. If the gates are open, leave them open; if they are closed, close them back. Do not chase or harass any livestock on the leases. Stay on the marked trail. Don't allow horses to damage any crops the trail may pass through by grazing or trampling. Even if there is no evidence of a crop in a plowed field, stay out of it. It may be newly seeded.
- Rowdy horseplay, racing or other forms of potentially dangerous behavior are unacceptable. Use common sense and courtesy while on Corps-managed trails.

Nearest Services:

Because this is a continuous trail it is difficult to say where the nearest services are. Food, gas, ice and picnic supplies can be found at most of the small towns and service stations along US 51, US 69 and US 412. Medical and veterinary services are available in Wagnor, Muskogee and Tulsa.

For Information Contact:

Webbers Falls Project Office
Route 2, Box 21
Gore, OK 74435
Phone: 918-489-5541

Chouteau Compound
Route 1, Box 75A
Porter, OK 74454
Phone: 918-687-6091

Maps available by contacting the Webbers Falls Project Office.

Lake Carl Blackwell Equestrian Trails

Overview:

Stillwater, the nearest town to Lake Carl Blackwell, has roots that run deep into the history of Oklahoma. It was the location of the most ambitious effort of the Boomer's to grab and hold land in Indian Territory before the Run of 1889. A small lake at the north edge of town still carries the name Boomer Lake. One of Stillwater's first acts as an incorporated city was to sell bonds for an Agricultural and Mechanical College. This makes Oklahoma State University, one of the oldest universities in the state. Many students from the university and equestrians from Stillwater take advantage of the horse trails that have been developed around Lake Carl Blackwell.

Location of the Trail:

Nine miles west of Stillwater on Hwy 5, you will see the entrance. Turn north and follow the blacktop road to the interior. If you are unable to get a permit at the gate you will have to go on to the lake office. A $3.00 permit is required for use of the primitive horse camp and trails.

Camp Facilities Summary:

Type: Day use or overnight camping
Fees: $3.00
Electric: None
Restrooms: None
Showers: None
Water: None

Trail Summary:

Type: Public use with minimum day use fee.
Terrain: Open pasture, some trees and woods. Most of the trail parallels the lakeshore.
Difficulty: Easy.
Length: These trails are not marked. You have to hunt and peck to find your way around unless you are fortunate enough to ride with a local rider

who knows the trails. **You can not ride all the way around the lake**. Because this is an out and back trail be sure to double your mileage to figure riding time.

Trail markers: None
Trail Maps: None

Trail Notes:

I drove down to the lake office for a permit. There is an easy place there to turn your trailer around. The office is the park grocery store. From there I followed the attendants instructions and went back to the first parking place for horse trailers. It is a large grassy pasture.

To find one section of the trail ride out the way you drove in. Cross the road and follow the ditch to the corner. Just around the corner you will see a rather narrow metal gate. Go through the gate and follow the trail. There were no markings at the time I was there.

Camp Rules and Responsibilities:

Do not tie horses to trees.
No loose or hobbled horses

Nearest Services:

Gas, Groceries, feed or veterinary care can be found as close as Stillwater just minutes away.

For More Information:

Lake Carl Blackwell
405-372-5157

Okmulgee Wildlife Management Area

Overview:

The Okmulgee area has a history typical of many Oklahoma areas. It consists of Native Americans and oil. Okmulgee's history began after the Creek tribal lands ceased to be held in communal ownership and the Creek Nation was opened to settlement. A ride through this wildlife management area give you a feeling of why this land was special to the Creek Indians who lived here.

Location of the Trail:

The trail head is located west of Okmulgee, north of Hwy 56. Once you are on Hwy 56 follow the signs to the wildlife management headquarters. Six miles past the Git n Go. Pass the Okmulgee Lake turnoff, pass the spillway. Right after the spillway on your right is a dirt road with a cattle guard. A brown sign says "Okmulgee GMA". Turn right and go up the hill. You will see the headquarters; if you have a large trailer it is better to stop out by the big tree. Walk in to ask for information. There isn't much room for turning trailers around inside the compound.

Camp Facilities Summary:

Type: Most of the time this area is day use. Sometimes you may camp overnight with permission of the local Ranger.
Fees: None
Electric: None
Restroom: None
Showers: None
Water: None

Trail Summary:

Type: Day use.
Terrain: Open pasture, some trees, woods, and a few (but not many) rocks.
Difficulty: Easy.

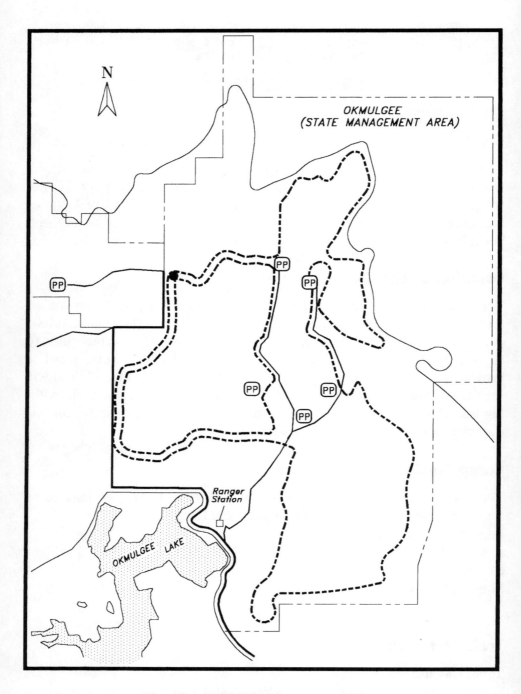

Okmulgee Wildlife Management Area

Length: Twenty-five miles marked.
Trail markers: Some markers on trees.
Trail Maps: Only what is available in the *Guide to Oklahoma Horse Trails*.

Trail Notes:

This trail was laid out for the Cougar Prowl Endurance ride. You will find many sections that are not only beautiful but fun, because you can canter for long distances without fighting rocks. It is flat and what the author calls a "fast track". The best part of the trail follows the Deep Fork River in some big bottomland hardwoods. These trees will make you stop and take another look. You can also ride two ridges, one gives a view of Okmulgee, the other lets you view Okmulgee Lake.

Trail Rules and Responsibilities:

Do not tie horses to trees.
Be sure to stay on the trail
No loose or hobbled horses
Park in designated areas.
All rules for riding in WLMA apply

Nearest Services:

All services can be found in Okmulgee which is approximately seven miles.

For More Information:

Oklahoma Department of Wildlife Conservation
P.O. Box 53465
Oklahoma City, OK 73105

Walnut Creek Equine Trails

Overview:

Walnut Creek State Park, west of Sand Springs, was established in 1964 by a dam on the Arkansas River that formed the sprawling Keystone Reservoir. Several small towns in the area were gobbled up by the lake. New settlements like New Prue have grown to meet the needs of tourists who want to enjoy the recreation provided by the lake.

Deep in the heart of Indian country, much of this area was once claimed by various tribes. With the rocks, hills, and trees to provide good cover, the Dalton gang often camped in the Keystone - Walnut Creek area. Some of the Dalton loot from a local bank robbery is said to be covered by Lake Keystone.

Location of the Trail:

Walnut Creek State Park is located on Keystone Lake, near Prue, off of Hwy. 412\64 (Cimarron Turnpike) west of Sand Springs, Oklahoma. Take the 209th West Street exit (also known as Prue Road) and go north about 13 1\2 miles. The park is on your left. After you turn in to the area you will see the park office on your left. Stay on this blacktop to area 2 section B, if you are planning overnight camping. Areas one and two A both have day-use parking.

Camp Facilities Summary:

Type: Day-use or overnight camping
Fees: There is no day use fee. It costs $11.00 for overnight camping without electric. There is an additional fee for electric.
Electric: Yes
Restroom: Yes, flush toilets
Showers: Yes, hot water
Water: Yes, for both people and horses.
 This is a very clean well kept camp with plenty of shade.

Trail Summary:

Type: Public use
Terrain: Open pasture, some trees, woods, and rocks. Pretty views of the lake.
Difficulty: Easy.
Length: There are two sections of trails. Each is an out and back from the overnight camp in area 2 B. Because this trail is new and some of it is still being marked it is better to ride this trail for time rather than distance. There are 15 miles available to ride at this time. If you know how fast your horse walks you can get an idea of how far you have ridden.
 Trail markers: Trails are marked with green and white ribbons. Loops or side trails are marked with blue and white or red and white.
Trail Maps: Yes, check with lake headquarters for latest information.

Trail Notes:

 The camp is big, open and well maintained. There is room for large trailers. Camp sites include picket polls, back in gravel pads, electric, water, cement picnic tables and charcoal grills. Shade is plentiful and there is usually a nice Oklahoma breeze. The camp includes hot showers, restroom fa-

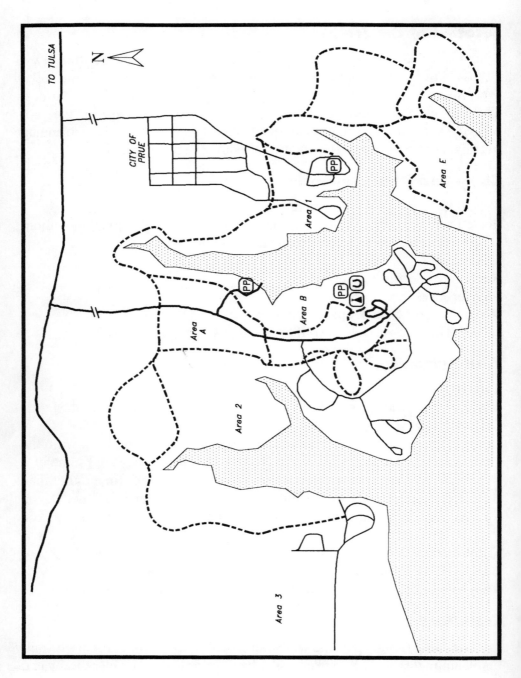

Walnut Creek State Park

cilities and a phone. For those who don't want to ride there is a place to swim and fish, plus there is a playground for children.

From the overnight camp area the trail goes north and then east around Walnut Creek Cove or north and then west around Rock Creek Cove. The trail east passes near some residential areas in a couple of place and it also goes near the city of New Prue. If you don't mind riding a couple a block on the road you can ride to a local convenience store for refreshments. Otherwise you need to be alert when riding through this section because it is easy to follow a local path to a backyard by mistake.

On the Walnut Creek leg of the trail, riders will find a great picnic site in a park that is closed to the vehicle public but open to equestrains. Some of the picnic tables are right at the waters edge. The west trail which loops around Rock Creek Cove also leads to a lake shore site.

These trails have all kinds of possibilities. It is a trail I will ride again. The campground was one of the best I stayed in Oklahoma.

Camp Rules and Responsibilities:

Do not tie horses to trees.
Be sure to stay on marked trail
Bag manure and hay and take it home with you
No loose or hobbled horses
No horses in comfort station, shelter or picnic areas except in designated Horse Camp.
NO RIDING ON BEACHES.
Be cautious of bogs in some areas.
Stallions must be well mannered and double-tied.
Generators in main camp will be turn off from 10 PM to 6 AM.
Absolutely no firearms or alcoholic beverages on trails.
Courtesy is the rule - in camp and on the trails.

Nearest Services:

Gas, groceries, and picnic supplies may be found in New Prue. Feed or veterinary care can be found in Sand Springs. Hospitals are available in Tulsa.

For More Information:

Walnut Creek State Park
918-242-3362

Will Rogers Country Centennial Trail

Overview:

Much of the recorded history of the Centennial Trail area began in the early 1800's. Lt. Zebulon Pike, followed the Arkansas River in 1810 and arrived in the Verdigris Valley somewhere in the vicinity of the Oologah Dam.

One of the first families to the area was Will Rogers' father, Clem V. Rogers a blood citizen of the Cherokee Nation. Clem Rogers built his house at the foot of an oak-crowned sandstone bluff overlooking a vast expanse of river bottom farmland. Will Rogers was born there November 11, 1879. The house was moved a mile west of its original location to avoid its destruction when the water basin filled behind the new dam. The house is located on the Dog Iron Ranch which was established by Clem Rogers before the Civil War. This house can be seen from many locations on the trail by looking to the northwest across the lake.

The first oil in the Indian Territory was discovered in this general area in 1889. Many of the towns in the vicinity have historical Indian names, for example, Oolagah, meaning Dark Cloud, was named for a Cherokee Chief. Other names can be looked up in local history i.e. Talala, Nowata, Coddy's Bluff, Bushyhead, and Catoosa, just to name a few.

Will Rogers' life took him from cattle ranges and Oklahoma hills to the vaudeville stage. He was a humorist loved by a nation. As a movie star he made more than 70 western films. As a columnist he reached more than 40 million readers a day. This trail was named in memory of Will. A rider has a good view of the home from Knight Hill but because of lake water levels it is often both difficult and unsafe to try to reach the hill.

Construction of the equestrian trail began in 1975 and was a cooperative effort of the Corps of Engineers and volunteers from the Oklahoma Equestrian Trail Riders Association.

Location of the Trail:

Will Rogers Country Centennial Trail has two trail heads. The first one is located near the lake's emergency spillway. Access is directly from SH 88 east of Oolagah. Because this trail is an "out and back" or a continuous trail the other trailhead is at the opposite end located in Blue Creek Park. The road to the Blue Creek Camp is well marked going in. Follow the signs from SH 88 each turn is marked.

Camp Facilities Summary:

No facilities exist at the Spillway trailhead. There is a gravel parking lot with no shade or water.

Will Rogers Equestrian Campground in Blue Creek RV park:
Type: Public, day use or overnight camping
Fees: $5.00 per campsite or $25.00 to reserve all eight campsites per night.
    To make reservations contact the Corp of Engineers.
Electric: None
Restrooms: Yes
Showers: Yes (however you have to drive down to the RV park which is
    about a quarter of a mile.
Water: Yes
Other: Direct access to the trail, group fire ring and picket posts, charcoal
    grill, a cement picnic table and gated security.

Trail Summary:

Type: Public
Fees: None if you are riding from the spillway.

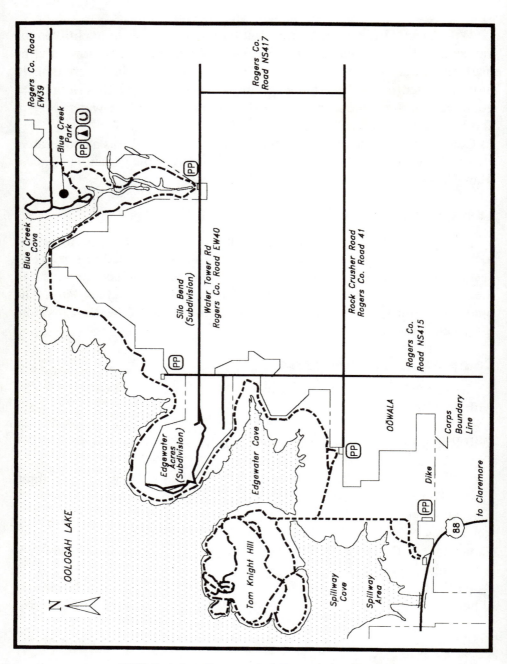

Will Rogers Centennial Equestrian Trail

Terrain: Open pasture, some trees. Much of this trail parallels the lake and part of it is directly on the lakeshore. Be sure to check with the Corp before riding in wet weather. This trail can get boggy.
Difficulty: Easy, if it is not rainy season.
Length: 18 miles if you get to include the trails on Frank Knight Hill.
Trail Markers: Karsonite posts.
Trail Maps: Yes, available on request or when you check into the horse camp.

Trail Notes:

Although the rest of the campground is winterized on September 30, and reopened on April 1, the equestrian campground is available year-round with fees (except during deer season). Primitive camping is allowed along the trail on a case by case basis, permission is required. Check with the Corp office to make arrangements.

I found this trail easy to ride and uniquely interesting. However, it can also be dangerous after high water. Some of the ground doesn't look boggy but is. Be sure to check with the appropriate Corp personnel before riding this trail during a rainy spell or after high water.

Actual trail construction was held to a minimum to protect the natural features of the land. I found most of the markers in place but if there is a "Y" leaving a question about which way to go, there is nothing to give you any indication about the correct direction. For example, shortly after leaving Blue Creek Campground you come to a "Y" intersection of the trail. If you turn left you find yourself at the camp entrance with no place to go but down the blacktop or onto private property. If you turn right and you end up at Blue Creek crossing. During dry weather this would be the appropriate choice. During wet weather forget it unless you like mud better than I do or unless your horse or mule does a good breast stroke.

The latest information from the from the Corp indicates some work has been done to make a deep ford less dangerous. When I visited this area both the mud and water looked too DEEP to interest me. I've been told that has changed. There is also plenty of road riding if you enjoy that. .

Nearest Services:

Camping and picnic supplies can be found at small convenience stores near the dam. The nearest veterinary or medical services can be found in Claremore which is approximately 12 miles.

THIS TRAIL IS A DRY WEATHER TRAIL.

For information contact:

Oologah Resident Office
Corps of Engineers
Route 1, Box 1610
Oolagah, Oklahoma 74053-9764
918-443-2250

Powwow Protocol

If you are a visitor to Oklahoma, your will likely have the opportunity to attend a contemporary intertribal powwow before you leave. A powwow is the coming together of Native American tribes for the purpose of singing, dancing, feasting, selling and trading arts and crafts and upholding traditional customs.

Visitors are welcome at intertribal powwows, although common courtesy dictates that all guests remain respectful of the Indian tradition and customs. Most such powwows do not provide seating. To be on the safe side bring your own lawn chair or blanket.

Guests may join the Round Dance or at the invitation of the emcee. Do not enter the dance floor to participate in the "Giveaway". It is important to remember the dance area is sacred. Women should wear shawls in the dance area.

If a powwow feast is served, visitors are welcome to eat after the staff has eaten. Bring your own plates and utensils. Do not sit on benches encircling the dance area or take flash photography during the contests. It is polite to ask dancers and singers before taking pictures.

Any questions pertaining to powwow protocol should be directed to the powwow emcee.

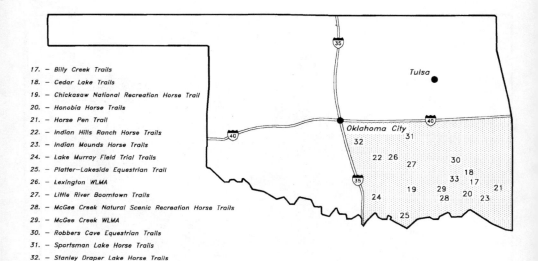

17. – Billy Creek Trails
18. – Cedar Lake Trails
19. – Chickasaw National Recreation Horse Trail
20. – Honobia Horse Trails
21. – Horse Pen Trail
22. – Indian Hills Ranch Horse Trails
23. – Indian Mounds Horse Trails
24. – Lake Murray Field Trial Trails
25. – Platter–Lakeside Equestrian Trail
26. – Lexington WLMA
27. – Little River Boomtown Trails
28. – McGee Creek Natural Scenic Recreation Horse Trails
29. – McGee Creek WLMA
30. – Robbers Cave Equestrian Trails
31. – Sportsman Lake Horse Trails
32. – Stanley Draper Lake Horse Trails
33. – Talimena Horse Trails

Oklahoma — Southeast

Billy Creek Trail

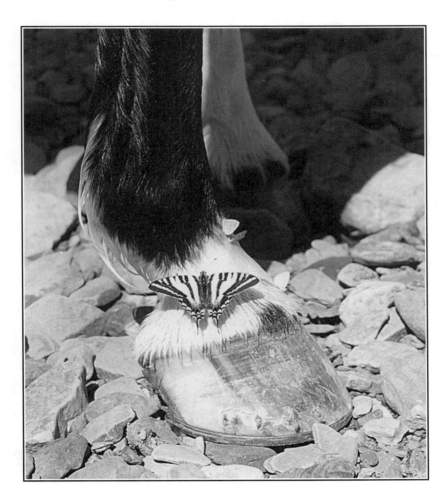

Overview:

At the junction of US 259 and OK 63 squats a little community known as Big Cedar. It is no metropolis not even a small village but it is well known because John F Kennedy spoke there. October 29th, two years before his assassination JFK came for the dedication of the U.S. Hwy 259 as a guest of Senator Robert S. Kerr. A monument to Kennedy occupies a place by the side of the road.

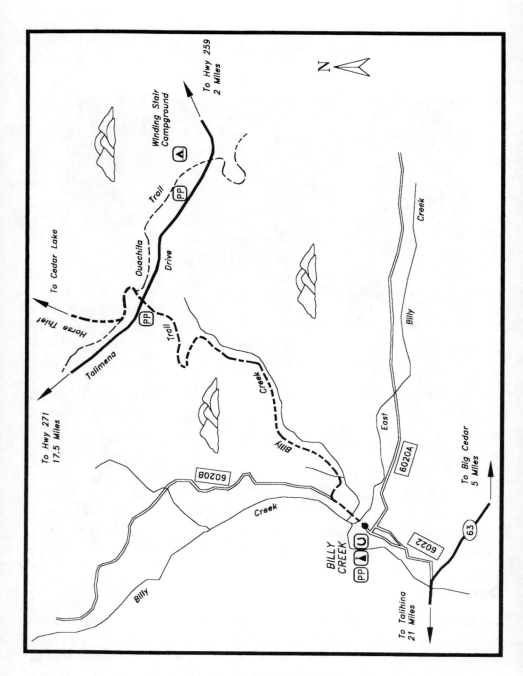

Billy Creek Horse Trail

The area is known as a sportsman's paradise. Choctaw, who were given the land, found it full of game and fish. During the pre-Civil War days trails through the region were used by prospectors whose searches for silver and gold went unrewarded.

Location of the Trail:

At the junction of US 259 and OK 63 take 63 west 5 miles. A sign reads Talimena Drive 10 miles and points to your right up the mountain. The turn is a very hard right if you are coming from Big Cedar. You are now on FR 6022 which is blacktop. Brown and cream colored signs point the way to Billy Creek Campground. After crossing a narrow one lane bridge the road turns to gravel.

Once your arrive at Billy Creek campground don't pull in. Horse trailers should follow FR 6020B. This is a narrow grey gravel road with a clear cut on the right. A few spindly pines tell the story of some past logging operation and barbed wire fences guard both sides of the road. Don't take 6020A, continue straight ahead into a flat parking area. Here you will see about 10 parking spots laid out on the diagonal and some hitching posts. This is where you saddle up.

When you come back out of the trailer spot and turn to your right you will see the trailhead bulletin board. Sign in here so rangers will know how many riders use this camp. Maps are usually available at this point.

Camp Facilities Summary:

Type: Public; day use camp area
Fees: None
Electric: None
Rest rooms: Yes across the road in the RV camp. (see water)
Showers: None
Water: Yes. You must go across the road to the RV camp ground. A slot built in the fence allows riders to walk through but you may not take your horses or mules.

Trail Summary:

Type: Public; equestrian and hikers
Terrain: Mountainous and rocky

Difficulty: From this camp the trail must be considered most difficult because it climbs up to Talimena Drive.
Length: 3.5 miles to the top. This is considered Billy Creek Trail; however, Billy Creek connects with Cedar Lake so you now have 40 miles of marked trail to ride.
Trail Markers: White and yellow rectangles on trees. Yellow is for the equestrians.

Trail Notes:

Billy Creek Trail serves both hikers and equestrians. The trail parallels the creek as it climbs out of Billy Creek Valley. The trail then travels along a scenic southern ridgeline of Winding Stair Mountain and crosses the Talimena Scenic Byway. One mile west of Winding Stair Campground, Billy Creek intersects the Ouachita National Recreation Trail. Take this trail either left or right to hook up with Cedar Lake Trails. Most of the people who ride this trail come from the Cedar Lake Equestrian Trails. However, if you are interested in joining the trails from this area you may camp overnight in the forest a short ways from Billy Creek parking area.

Rules and Regulations:

Don't drink from streams or ponds.
Use rocky areas to cross steams and wet areas.
Scatter hay and manure when camping along the trail.
Use treesaver straps. Don't tie directly to trees.
Pack it in...Pack it out.

Nearest Services:

Services to this area are limited. Big Cedar is the closest but that would be mostly for gas and snacks. Talihina is about 25 miles.

For More Information:

Choctaw Ranger District
HC 64, Box 3467
Heavener, OK 74937
(918) 653-2991

Cedar Lake Equestrian Trails

Overview:

Enhanced by the Kiamichi and Winding Stair Mountains 90-acre Cedar Lake provides the backdrop for one of the premiere horse trails in the nation. This campground is one of the few areas which has been extensively developed by the U.S. Forest service for the Equestrian community. It serves as a prototype for other equestrian campgrounds throughout the country.

Location of Trail:

To find Cedar Lake Equestrian Camp drive 10 miles south of Heavener, OK on U.S. Hwys 270\59 to Holson Valley Road. As you drive toward Cedar Lake from Heavener, you will cross a valley and start up a hill. Some where near the bottom of this hill you will see a sign - DANGER rifle range. Use this sign as a signal for your next turn. When you see a small brown and white sign for Cedar Lake turn right and continue 3 miles to the park. Turn right again and follow the signs to the equestrian area.

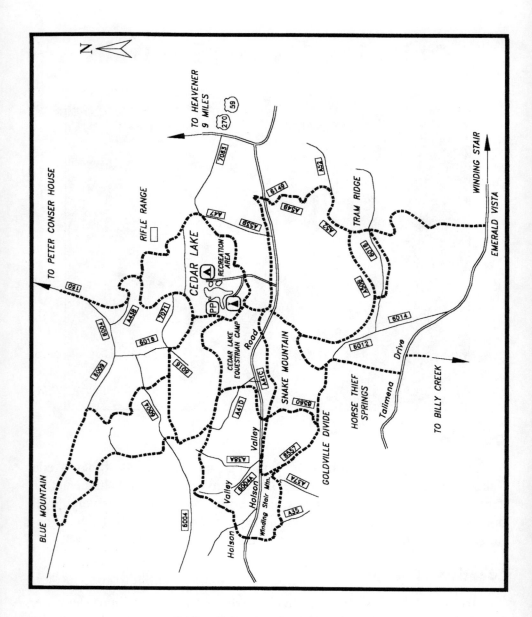

Cedar Lake Equestrian Trails

Camp Facilities Summary:

Type: Public, day use and overnight camping
Fees: Camping fees vary according to the type of campsite your choose. The more services you want, the more it costs. The most expensive site is a double which costs $12.00 a night.
Electric: Yes, 28 sites have both water and electric
Restrooms: Yes, flush toilets
Showers: Yes, hot water.
Water: Yes, for both people and horses

Trail Summary:

Type: Public use with camping fee
Terrain: Forested, hilly with rocks. Trails are rated as easy, more difficult and most difficult. The ratings reflect the degree of slope, roughness of footing, trail width, and how well vegetation has been cleared for ease of riding.
Difficulty: Each loop may be different according to the criteria already mentioned.
Length: The trails are set up in loops so you may set your own length for each ride. There are 70 plus miles of marked trails.
Trail Markers: Yellow rectangular blazes on trees.
Other Activities: Hiking, biking, swimming, fishing.

Trail Notes:

Signs strategically placed around the Equestrain camping area show where to access the trails. Yellow rectangular blazes on trees mark the horse\mules trails. White blazes signify hiker's trails and blue is the Ouachita National Recreation Trail which is a "no-no" for equestrians. A trail circles the whole camp. This gives riders access to their parking pads without having to ride through the center of camp.

Everyone has special places they like to go on the Cedar Lake Trail system. Understanding that the thrill of discovery is part of the fun of riding trail, Horse Thief Springs, Billy Creek Trailhead and Peter Conser's House are three places you may want to discover.

Horse Thief Springs was first made famous by the outlaw, Belle Starr, who lived near the small town of Porem, OK. Bell was known as a good judge of horse flesh and she coveted horses that belonged to other folks as much as she coveted her own. Belle set up a series of stations 50 miles apart to exchange stolen horses from one area to another. Horses stolen in Texas were sold in Arkansas and Horses stolen in Arkansas were moved to Texas. Horses Thief Springs was noted as one of those stopover watering holes. The spring is located on trail # 9.

The Billy Creek Trailhead is the farthest point south on the trail system at the time this was written. Use trail # 7 from Winding Stair Campground or trail # 9 from Horse Thief Springs. Billy Creek provides access to the Cedar Lake Trail system for day-use riders coming from Hwy. 63 out of Big Cedar. This camp is primitive. No facilities of any kind except hitching posts. The parking area is flat, level and will accommodate about 10 trailers. Potable water and restroom facilities are available across the road in Billy Creek RV campground. Horses are not welcome there, however, a slot in the fence allows people to walk through.

A third point of interest to discover is Peter Conser's house. Although it might not be designated clearly on the map you can ride directly to this historic site. Only about two miles of the ride is on a lightly used road, the rest is on trails.

Peter Conser was a well-known Choctaw Lighthorseman who become a deputy sheriff of the Choctaw Nation at age twenty-five. Later, he became captain in the Choctaw Lighthorse Mounted Police. In the 1820's these mounted police were sheriff, judge, jury and executioner for the Five Civilized Tribes. Prominent in the local business community, Conser owned and operated a farm, gristmill, general store, and sawmill. His 19th century home, now a museum, has been restored to reflect the family's wealth and social position.

Information from the Forest Service suggests the following combinations of loops:

Post Mountain Loop

This is a combination of trail # 1 and # 2. An 8 mile trip leads travelers over rolling terrain and two creek crossings. After storms, these creeks can become difficult to cross. Both trails are rated more difficult.

Holson Valley Loop

Trails # 4, # 4a and # 5 provide a 7.5 mile trip. this is a leisurely ride through the Homer L. Johnson Wildlife Management Area. A quiet ride through this area will give you a good opportunity to view wildlife in its natural habitat.

Red Lick
Trails # 5, # 5a and # 6 provide a 15 mile trip. This loop follows ridgelines and overlooks the Red Lick Drainage. The trail will cross Cedar Creek twice at the northwest end and Red Lick Creek at the northeast end. These three trails are rated more difficult.

Emerald Vista
Trails # 6 and # 7 create a 16.5 mile trip. These two trails cover steep terrain with long grades. You will ride through two drainages ending at the top of Winding Stair Mountain. Trail # 6 is rated more difficult and Trail # 7 is most difficult.

Blue Mountain
Trails # 2 and # 8 make a 15.5 mile trip that begins at camp. This ride includes an unforgettable view from the site of an old fire tower. The west loop of trail # 8 is very steep and rated most difficult. Trail # 2 is rated more difficult.

Goldville Route
The loop connects # 3 to # 6 and # 7. Goldville Divide area was named from an old goldmine. Much of this ride is easy and along roads.

Camp Rules and Trail Responsibilities:

On the Trail:
Prevent erosion by using rocky areas to cross streams and wet areas.
Avoid cutting switchbacks. Ride on designated areas.
Scatter hay and manure when camping along the trail.
Use tree saver straps. Don't tie horses directly to trees.
Even though the trails are well marked you should carry a map and compass.
Tell someone where you plan to ride and when you plan to be back.
Carry matches and flashlights in case of an emergency.

In Camp:
Rake and pile manure for easy removal by pickup crews.
Tie horses to your trailer or use tree savers. Do not tie directly to trees.

You may use picket poles.
At some campsites portable corrals are also allowed.
Quiet hours between 10:30 pm and 6:30 am.

If you plan to ride at Cedar Lake during the peak season from March through October, it is a good idea to call ahead for reservations. To make reservations call 10 days in ADVANCE. 1-800-280-2267.

Nearest Services:

Most of the time there is a small store in the park. This store has ice and picnic supplies. You can also enjoy a cafe. Small operations such as this are sometimes seasonal and change hands periodically. If you plan to count on it for meals better call ahead and check the status.

Other services such as gas, groceries, feed or veterinary is 10 miles away at Heavener on U.S. 270\59.

For Information:

Forest Service
Choctaw Ranger District
HC 64, Box 3467
Heavener, OK 74937
Phone: 918-653-2991

Topos or Area Maps
Trail maps are available at the Equestrian Camp. Topos can be purchased at the newspaper office in Heavener Oklahoma.

Chickasaw National Recreation Horse Trails

Overview:

Proclaimed the land of "smelly waters." Indians knew about the many mineral springs that bubbled from the earth in the vicinity of Sulphur long before a white man set foot in Oklahoma. But true to form, early white visitors to the area extolled the medicinal virtues of the sulphur scented water and a town was born. By 1895, a store housed a post office and the community was called Sulphur Springs. Hotels and rooming houses blossomed to tend to the needs of the tourists who came to "take the waters." Bromide Spring was "nationally known as a sure cure for nervous diseases and stomach troubles." Bromide Springs has since dried up but Pavilion and Black Sulphur springs are still flowing strong near the park's entrance.

Location of the Trail:

The trailhead is located west of Veterans Lake in the Chickasaw National Recreation Area. From Hwy 7 in Sulphur take 12 street south to the recre-

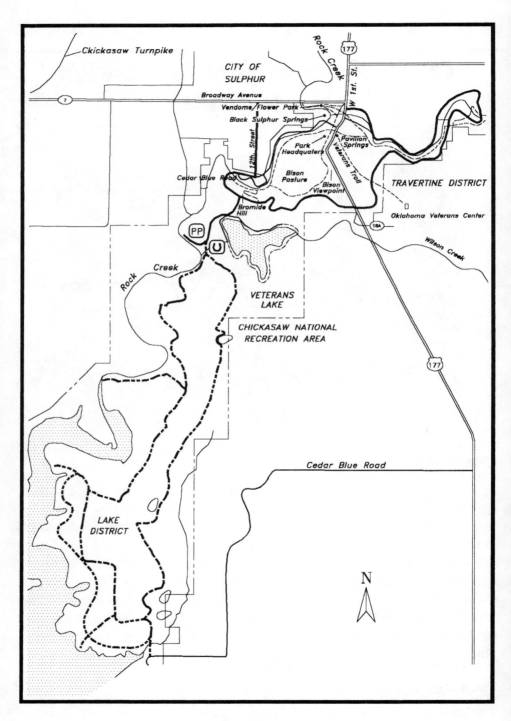

Chickasaw National Recreation Area

ation area entrance. Turn right on the first road and continue until you see a sign that says Veterans Lake and take another right. It is hard to tell when you are at the trailhead because there isn't much there to indicate where to park. Parking is beside the road anywhere near the trailhead. Look to the left as you drive along behind the dam. When you see and iron gate across a trail you are there.

Camp Facilities Summary:

Type: Public, day use
Fees: None
Electric: None
Restroom: None
Showers: None
Water: None

Trail Summary:

Type: Day use.
Terrain: Open pasture, some trees, woods, and a few but not many rocks.
Difficulty: Easy.
Length: Fifteen miles.
Trail Markers: Some markers on trees. Some piles of rocks. Some not marked at all.
Trail Maps: Only what is available in the *Guide to Oklahoma Horse Trails*.

Trail Notes:

The trails are natural and follow ridges, cross small valleys and follow along creek beds. Huge red cedars dot the open areas and give the trail an excuse to turn. Elm, cottonwood and oak are scattered through the valleys. Springs, streams and lakes – water has always been the attraction at Chickasaw National Recreation Area. Rock Creek makes no exception. Not only is it a watering place for you horse or mule, it is a great place to wet your feet and cool off on a hot summer ride. The trail which is about 15 miles long, winds along one arm of the Lake of the Arbuckles.

Trail Rules and Responsibilities:

Do not tie horses to trees.
Be sure to stay on the trail
No loose or hobbled horses

Nearest Services:

All services can be found in Sulphur.

For More Information:

Superintendent, Chickasaw National Recreational Area
PO Box 201,
Sulphur, OK 73068

Traveler's Information

Average High Temps

March 62	August 93
April 72	Sept 85
May 79	October 70
June 87	Nov 62
July 93	Dec. Jan. Feb. 45 to 55

Daylight Savings Time
From the last week of October to the first week of April

Central Standard Time
May through to the end of the third week of October.

State Tourist Information
800-652-6552

Highway Patrol
405-682-4343

Road & Weather Conditions
405-425-2385

Honobia Horse Trails

Overview:

The community of Honobia is isolated in the Kiamichi Mountains. Pioneers, Indians, gold prospectors and outlaws all trod the trails of the Kiamichis. The land was know for its beauty and solitude, as well as, its plentiful wildlife. Today's trails still provide the same beauty little has changed since the land belonged to the Choctaw. Kent Perkins provides the opportunity for modern day equestrians to ride these historical trails.

Location of Trail:

Take U.S. 271 south from Clayton to State Hwy 144. Follow this blacktop until it ends. Then follow the signs. When you turn in at the camp, stop at the office located on the right and someone will give you directions on where to park your trailer.

Camp Summary:

Type: Private campground
Fees: Yes. Call for information.
Electric: Yes
Restrooms: Yes, flush toilets
Showers: Yes, hot water
Water: Yes, both people and horses

Trail Summary:

Type: Private
Terrain: mountainous.
Difficulty: This depends on the trails you choose.
Length: This is generally set by the trail-guide.

Trail Notes:

These rides are generally set up as large group rides, however, you can set up smaller private rides by calling to make reservations with Kent. Wild

Horse Trail Rides sponsors about five rides a year -- April, May, September, October and December. Ride costs vary. Call for information.

Rules and Responsibilities:

Check at the Office.

Nearest Services:

The nearest camping supplies, gas, groceries and restaurants can be found in Clayton. Major services such as hospitals and vet can be found in McAlister or Hugo.

For Information Contact:

Kent Perkins
P.O. Box 70
Honobia, OK 74549
918-755-4466
Fax: 918-755-4577

Horse Pen Trail

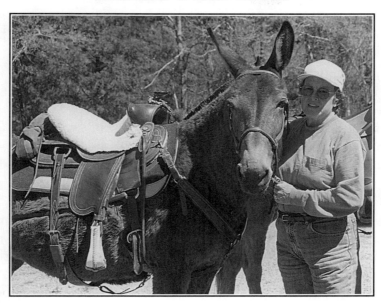

Overview:

Horse Pen Trail is actually a small camp at the edge of the Oklahoma-Arkansas border. The area is in the Ouachita National Forest and is on the perimeter of the Kiamichi Wilderness. This area in the past has been known for barrel staves, Choctaw Indians, fabulous scenery and wildlife. The area is known as a sportsman's paradise. Choctaw who were given the land found it full of game and fish.

Location of the Trail:

In Big Cedar at the junction of US 259 and OK 63, take 63 east until you see the Horse Pen sign. Turn left on a narrow road and follow it 6/10's of a mile. The road often has muddy looking tracks in it, but the bottom is rock so you don't have too much to worry about.

Camp Facilities Summary:

Type: Public; day use camp area
Fees: None
Electric: None

Rest rooms: None
Showers: None
Water: None

Trail Summary:

Type: Public; equestrian, hikers and hunters
Terrain: Mountainous and rocky
Difficulty: Most difficult
Length: Choose your own. This camp is on the edge of a wilderness area. No marked trails.
Trail Markers: None

Trail Notes:

I have been to this camp. It is open and inviting although camping is primitive. Looking at the surrounding area, it seems a person who likes brush busting or cross country travel, would love it. Although I have not ridden in this particular area I have experienced several other wilderness areas. These are not for the faint of heart or the novice. If you plan to ride in primitive wilderness area plan to travel for low impact and don't go unless you have a good understanding of how to read a map and compass.

Rules and Regulations:

Don't drink from streams or ponds.
Use rocky areas to cross streams and wet areas.
Use treesaver straps. Don't tie directly to trees.
Pack it in...Pack it out.

Nearest Services:

Services to this area are limited. Big Cedar is the closest but that would be mostly for gas and snacks. Heavener, OK or Mena, AR will be able to provide more services.

For More Information:

Choctaw Ranger District
HC 64, Box 3467
Heavener, OK 74937
918-653-2991

Indian Hills Ranch Horse Trails

Overview:

Tribbey is what remains of an agricultural trading center. In 1904, the year after the Santa Fe railroad came the population began to grow. During harvest time the people often numbered upwards of 200. It doubled by 1912. Alpheus M. Tribbey managed the Tribbey House a residence hotel. King cotton was the big crop. There was a wagon yard where a man could board himself and his team for $1.50 a night. Cotton is no longer a major crop but you can still find a good place to spend the night with your horse at Indian Hills Ranch.

Location of Trail:

From I-40 just west of Shawnee, OK take the Dale exit (Hwy 102 south). This is also exit 178. Go 19 miles to Tribbey. The town is small so pay attention. The turn comes up before you expect it. Watch for a narrow red gravel road just before you reach the convenience store, then turn right. This is Slaughterville Rd. The back end of a semi-trailer that is permanently parked in the convenience store parking lot has a sign on it pointing west toward the ranch. Follow this road for about 1 1\2 miles to a "Y". Take the left fork and continue. A black and white sign points you in the right direction. The ranch entrance is a 1 1\2 miles down the road on the left.

You may also reach the ranch by taking Hwy 9 to Hwy 102-south and going 10 miles to Slaughterville Rd. Then do the same as described before. Or from the I-35 Percell exit take Hwy 39-E approximately 2 miles to Hwy 77. Go north on this road to Slaughterville Rd. Follow it east 15 miles and the ranch camp is on the right.

Camp Summary:

Type: Day use or overnight camping
Fees: Camping fees may change from year to year. Call for information.
Electric: Yes
Restrooms: Yes, flush toilets
Showers: Yes, hot water
Water: Yes, both people and horses

Trail Summary:

Type: Private Campground. There is a charge for camping and riding the trails. Call for current charges.
Terrain: Red hills and pastures. No rocks, some trees.
Difficulty: Easy
Length: The trails circle and criss cross pastures. Set your own mileage.
Trail Markers: Different color ribbons.
Maps: Maps are available at camp.

Trail Notes:

Because the owner does not allow hunting, you never know what kind of animals you might encounter. I saw a pack of five coyotes, five deer on various parts of the ranch, a covey of quail, a flock of ducks and one badger. If you are a bird watcher, as well as, a trail rider this place may very well be paradise. It is full of birds of all kinds.

The ranch and trails are divided by Slaugheterville Road. The terrain is easy. The trails are basically flat with a few draws and at least one small creek crossing on each side of the road. All trails can be accessed easily from the campground. Probably, the highlight of a day-ride is the opportunity to ride into the town of Tribbey for a cold drink and a snack. With hitching racks behind the convenience store, all the place lacks is a swinging door, then it could be the old west revisited.

Three or four swinging ride-through gates make it easy to get from one pasture to another. You need to remember this is a working cow ranch. If you open a gate be sure it shuts behind you.
On the farthest trail in the north pasture be aware of badger holes. It is a straight away and you will be tempted to gallop. Watch for the holes.

Rules and Responsibilities:

Do not tie horses directly to trees.
If gates are open leave them open. If they are shut be sure to shut them.

Nearest Services:

The nearest camping supplies, gas, groceries and restaurants can be found in Tribbey. Major services can be found in Shawnee or Oklahoma City.

For Information Contact:

Indian Hills Ranch
Rt. 2 Box 159 AB
Wanette, OK. 74878
405-899-4296

Indian Mounds Horse Trails

Overview:

A camp ground has been developed and opened to the public in Southeastern Oklahoma near Clayton. Located in the scenic Kiamichi Mountains, the camp is situated on the site of an ancient Indian Village. The mounds, all that remains of their early lodging places, are clearly visible throughout camp.

The mountains that surround the camp have taken their name from French word Kiamichi which means 'horned screamer'. It is believed early French trappers may have given this name to the Lesser Horned Owl or Screech Owl, which is frequently found in the area. The peaceful trails beckon both hikers and horsemen. Large rock formations, springs and vistas provide spectacular scenery. The trails vary from old abandoned logging trails to forest roads. Many are single file wooded trails.

For the equestrian, the camp is always open. You and your horse or mule are welcome anytime. Feel free to ride on your own or with a guided group. Maps are available at the camp and new trails are added frequently.

The camp is also available for group activities, trail rides, church outings, gospel sings, bluegrass festivals, etc. Bring your family, your horses, your boat and your camping gear. You'll find something to enjoy in Kiamichi country.

Location of Trail:

Indian Mounds Camp is located 2 miles southeast of Clayton, Oklahoma on US Hwy 271, then turn north 1/2 mile. When you come down the highway you will see blue and white camping signs that will guide you to camp. Blacktop roads provide easy access.

Camp Summary:

Type: Day use or overnight camping
Fees: Camping fees vary according to what services you want. Electric is $5.00 per night per site in addition to a camping fee. If you don't use electric you can camp for $5.00 per night plus $1.00 per person. Charges are different for various special events. It is always best to call for fee information.
Electric: Yes, 70 plus sites
Restrooms: Yes, flush toilets

Showers: Yes, hot water
Water: yes, both people and horses

Trail Summary:

Type: Private, there is a charge for camping, no charge for riding the trails.
Terrain: Forested, hilly with rocks.
Difficulty: Trails are easy, moderate or challenging.
Length: You can choose long, short or in-between. There are more than 100 miles of marked trails. The trails clover-leaf back to camp, with optional return routes. There are trails for every rider. You choose the degree of difficulty and the length.
Trail Markers: Different color ribbons.
Maps: Maps are available at camp.
Other Activities: Horse packing, Hiking, Photography, Fishing (nearby) and Hunting

Trail Notes:

All trails leave from the east side of camp. There are many interesting place to see such as Dennis Rock, the Lookout, and McKennley Rock. The trails are marked in different colors with surveyor ribbon to correspond with the map. There are many different loops, long or short, easy or difficult, trails or roads, to satisfy any rider. Water is available along most portions of the trails. It is recommended horses be shod due to the rocky terrain.

Some areas of the trail are steep and rocky while others are easy enough for the beginning horse or rider. Between Dennis Rock and Iron Spring on the organge loop it is crooked, rocky and very steep. The rise is from flat to 681 feet in a very short distance. Powder puffs of bright green moss and pale blue swatches of lichen decorate the rocks. The area offers a wide variety of plants and trees. It seems as if something is blooming nearly year round.

Wildlife is plentiful in the area. Many of the Oklahoma mammals can be seen here by the alert observer. Hunting for deer and turkey is allowed during fall months. Check with the Oklahoma Department of Wildlife, or Fish and Game regarding hunting seasons before traveling to Kiamichi between October and December.

Camp Rules and Responsibilities:

Do not tie horses directly to trees.
Pile all the manure and hay near the road for easy pick up.

Nearest Services:

The nearest camping supplies, gas, groceries and restaurants can be found in Clayton. Major medical and veterinary services are available in McAlester, Oklahoma or Paris, Texas (approximately 75 miles). Clayton does have a volunteer fire department with EMTs and a new vet just north of town.

For Information Contact:

Jess Johnson
Indian Mounds Camp
HC 60, Box 62
Clayton, OK 74536
918-456-6031

Health Related Matters

In 1996, Oklahoma passed a law which requires that horses have a coggins test within the last 12 months. You are also required to show a negative coggins whenever you attend any public event with your horse. This means pleasure ride, rodeo, parade.

To enter the state visitors are required to bring a current health certificate and negative coggins taken within the last 12 months (no copies)

Because such rules change regularly and without notice to prevent problems you may call 405-524-6404 this is the Department of Livestock Permits.

Lake Murray Field Trial Horse Trails

Overview:

Lake Murray and Lake Murray State Park were named for the colorful governor, William H. "Alfalfa Bill" Murray. The state park is the largest in Oklahoma and was created in 1933. A 5,200 acre reservoir nestled in wooded, rolling hills is a peaceful place to regroup and catch your breath from the every day world. Yet for all its tranquility, this lake is the hub of recreational activity. The bird dog field trial event is only one of the many activities held in the area. However, it is because of the field trials, horsemen come. The section of land which has been set aside for the dog trials is primitive, quiet and full of trails.

Location of the Trail:

From I-35 take Exit 29 east on U.S.Hwy 70. Turn right on Scenic Hwy 77. Proceed about a quarter of a mile. The park office is on the right. Just beyond the park office drive a sign announces Group Camp # 2. Turn left and follow the blacktop for two miles. Before you get to the group camp you will see a large barn and dog kennels on you left. This is the designated parking and camping area for riders using the field trial trails.

Coming from the east follow Hwy 70 to a four way stop at the intersection of U.S. Hwy 70 and Scenic Hwy 77. Turn left and follow the same directions as above.

Camp Facilities Summary:

Type:Day use and overnight camping.
Fees: None at this time.
Electric: Yes
Restrooms: Yes, flush toilets
Showers: Yes.
Water: Yes
Indoor stalls and small outdoor pens are available.

Trail Summary:

Type: Public, when field dog trails are not having an event.
Terrain: Open pasture, some trees, and woods. Some of the trail parallels the lakeshore.
Difficulty: Easy
Length: This is an open area, how far you ride is up to you.
Trail Markers: None
Trail Maps: None

Trail Notes:

The Lake Murray trails are open and pretty. You can ride across pastures, through areas with acattered trees and if you want, you can ride in the woods.

The terrain is flat with a few rolling hills. From most of the hilltops you have a great view of the lake. The area is large and you are free to choose which direction you wish to ride. The trails are not marked, so be sure to sellect landmarks that will help you find you way back to camp.

Camp Rules and Responsibilities:

This is a special use area for hunters and hunting dogs. The field trials run very regularly from September through April. Bird dog trials have priority over any other function. If you plan to ride during the regular use period call and check with the ranger in charge. That way you can avoid traveling a long ways, only to be disappointed.

When you leave please rake and remove all your hay and manure from the stalls. Please be courteous to the next camper. In this particular area we are guests. Treat the opportuntiy to ride here as a privilege.

Nearest Services:

All necessary services can be found in Ardmore. This includes veterinary, groceries, hospital etc. Picnic supplies and ice can be found at the four-way stop corner store.

For more information:

Park Office
405/223-4044

Platter-Lakeside Equestrian Trails
Lake Texoma

Overview:

Lake Texoma has 93,000 acres of surface and 580 miles of shore line. The lake is situated on the border between Texas and Oklahoma. Two wildlife areas help preserve the natural beauty around the lake.

The Platter Equestrian Trails on Lake Texoma are out and back. You can ride from the Lakeside trailhead or from Platter Flats. The author was told that most equestrians come from the Platter area. Because the author had camped at Lakeside, the trail is described from that trailhead.

Location of the Trail:

To get to Lakeside follow U.S. Hwy. 70 west from Durant to the Lakeside Recreation Area sign. Turn south and proceed to the Recreation area gate. However, **don't** enter. Turn left at the fence. There is a gravel road that exits the small turn-around area that you find yourself in. Follow this road until it deadends at the lake. Don't enter any formal looking campground you pass. Stay to the left. The horse camp area at this trailhead is primitive with a capital P.

To access the trail from the Platter primitive camp, take Hwy 75 to Platter exit. From Platter follow the signs to Platter Flats.

Camp Facilities Summary:

Type: Public; day or overnight use
Fees: None
Electric: None
Showers: None
Water: There is no people water; you can get horse water from the lake.

Trail Summary:

Type: Public
Terrain: Heavily wooded areas of oak and hickory, interspersed with some open meadows. There are a couple of creek crossings and one train track to traverse. Poison Oak and ivy is plentiful.

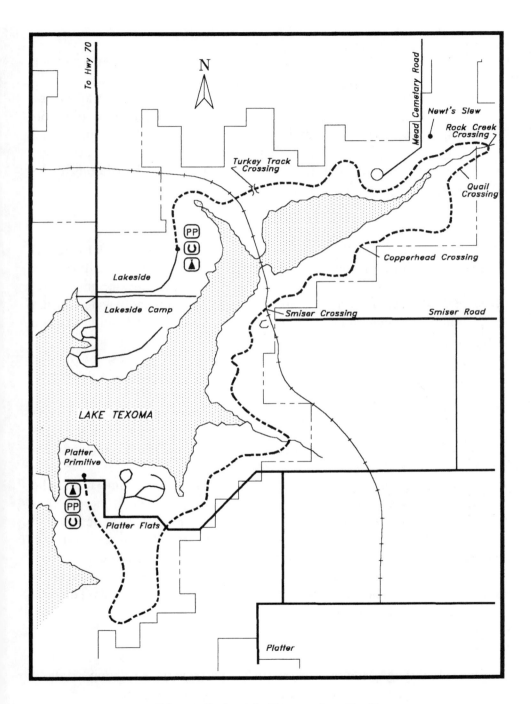

Platter-Lakeside Equestrian Trails

Difficulty: Easy in dry weather.
Length: 15 miles from one trail head to the other. If you ride out and back double your mileage.
Trail Markers: It seems a lot of people have helped mark this trail at one time or another. There is yellow and white, red and white, pink, orange and some blue. I put the most trust in the old yellow and white, and red and white ribbons. They are sometimes hard to see but they do mark the correct trails. Who cares what color the ribbons are as long as they get you where you want to go.

Trail Notes:

There is nothing to tell you where the trail begins. If you look to the left of where you came in you can see a metal pipe gate and a walk or ride through gate. Just on the other side you will pick up the trail ribbons. About 10 minutes out of camp there is a large gully you might want to watch during wet weather. I've been told there is a couple of places along this trail that run deep in the wet season.

The trail goes through some fairly dense thickets. Passes under large boid'arc and very old hardwood trees. These trees are old enough to definitely catch your attention.

15 minutes out of camp there is a deep creek crossing. It has no water or even mud during the dry season but you can tell it rolls high when the rains come. There is a rocky bottom which is a plus but I'm sure this place would get too deep for safe crossing in wet weather.

Turkey Track railroad crossing gives you a moment to think. It must be quite an experience to be near that track when a train passes. After you cross the tracks you will pick up a four wheeler trail. Watch closely for old ribbons and stay to the left, do not go to your right. That trail travels down there about 200 yards and dumps you in some weeds on the wrong side of the fence.

The trails on the north side of the track seem to be kept pretty clear by the four wheelers. The trails are a little wider and a little higher. This is a great place for cantering, very few, if any rocks.

Trail Rules:

Place all garbage and unburnable trash in garbage bags and deposit them in the trash cans provided at the entrance to the primitive area.

All loose hay and droppings should be scattered in the area.

Horses must be tied to the trailer or picket line at all times when in camp. Do not tie to trees.

Trail riders must stay on the trails and off public roadways.

Horses should remain off the trail during deer hunting season. Anyone insisting on riding during this period should protect themselves with blaze orange. Hang a few orange ribbons from your horse too. And you might add a bell.

Horses should be ridden at a walk in the primitive camp.

Watch for bogs along the lake shoreline when watering your horse.

The biggest concern when riding this trail is the danger of high water after a prolonged rain. If you are in doubt contact lake officials for more information before trying to ride in the area.

Nearest Services:

Groceries, feed, veterinary and health care can be found in Durant. Picnic supplies can be purchased at various convenience stores near the lake.

For more information:

Texoma Resident Office
P.O. Box 60
Cartwright, OK 74731
903-465-4990

Lexington Wildlife Management Area

Overview:

Lexington's reputation as the oldest town in Oklahoma Territory also gives rise to its reputation as rowdy, brawling, booze capital where a person could get away with anything. Estimates of the number of saloons vary from twenty-one to thirty. (Fugate, 1991) However, when Oklahoma came into statehood dry, the town settle into some hard times. But Lexington has survived fire, flood, and prohibition. Lexington WLMA is near Lexington on Slaughterville Rd.

Location of the Trail:

From Lexington take Hwy 77 north for approximately five miles. When the highway makes a jog left toward Noble you should see Slaughterville Rd going right or due east. Follow this road for about 5 1\2 miles. You will go by a church on the left and the WLMA office will be on your right. Turn in there and proceed across a cattle guard. You won't go far and you will see a nice wide flat parking area with some trash barrels. This is the staging area.

Trail Summary:

Type: WLMA; no riding during hunting seasons.
Terrain: Open pasture and woods. Some road riding.
Difficulty: Easy
Length: No specific length. Trails are unmarked.

Trail Notes:

When it is not hunting season equestrians are welcome to ride pretty much any where they want in this area. It is open grass and trees. Some trails are back off the road. In some parts it is easier to ride the roads. But even at that these are backwoods roads and not used a great deal. It is a good area for gaited folks to move out. Riders should be aware there is a correctional facility on the back side of this WLMA. When you leave it is probably best to go back the direction you came. The road gets pretty rough before you get to Tribbey if you try to drive on through that way.

Rules and Responsibilities:

Rules are often posted when you pull in to a WLMA. Please obey all rules. Riding in these areas are a big plus for the equestrian. One bad incident can block all riders out of an area. Be a good example.

Nearest Services:

Lexington or Noble have most service.

For More Information:

Oklahoma Department of Wildlife Conservation
P.O. Box 53465
Oklahoma City, OK 73105
405-521-2739

Little River Boomtown Trails

Overview:

Looking at the quiet wide spot in the road that stretches the imagination to be called a town, one could hardly guess at Maud's gloomy violent history. During the late 1890's in a nearly lawless land, mobs gathered quickly. Good judgement was seldom the name of the game. One such gathering led to the death of two young Indian boys and the arrest of 76 men, five of whom went to prison. Emotions ran so deep, one man was gunned down on the street of Maud after he returned from prison.

Riding past old oil well sites jump starts one's imagination. You can almost hear the hustle and bustle caused by the oil boom. The Discovery Well, famous in the area, produced 14,000 barrels a day under natural pressure. Pipes and cables, rusty memorials to another time, creep through the tall grass giving riders cause to be vigilant. In the bottom of a deep draw the trail passes a Model A Ford with a tree growing through the roof. What stories it could tell!

Location of the Trail:

From I-40 take Hwy 99 south to Seminole, OK. Continue to follow Hwy 99 south for 9 miles. Measure that nine miles from the railroad tracks on the south side of town. Turn left at E-W 133. Landmarks are a railroad car in the pasture on your left and a red and white stripped building. Go 1 1\2 miles to N-S 357. Turn left again or north and follow this road for about a mile and a half. The pasture is on the right. You will see trailers, a sign or the picnic shelters on your right.

Camp Facilities Summary:

Type: Private; day use; by reservation
Fees: Yes; fees vary by event
Electric: None
Rest rooms: Chemical toilets
Showers: None
Water: People none; there is a pond for the animals
Parking: Plenty of room for longest trailers

Trail Summary:

Type: Private; day use by reservation
Terrain: Flat, grasslands, some woods, creeks and river crossings.
Difficulty: Easy
Length: 15 miles
Trail Markers: Ribbons

Trail Notes:

The Boomtown trails begin in the House pasture where they have constructed open shelters with picnic tables for the riders to gather around for visiting and sharing snacks or lunch. The pasture is open with plenty of room for parking even if you pull a long trailer. A pond just over the hill provides plenty of water for the animals but you need to bring your own people water.

The work on the trails testify to the effort Pete House made to provide for good rides. He cut, trimmed and marked trail through some very scenic Oklahoma landscape. Trails traverse river bottoms, pass through black jack oak thickets and roll across green pastures. Some scenic spots like a huge natural rock formation in a patch of wild flowers, river crossings and the natural springs make you reach for your camera.

Rides at Little River Boomtown are usually group rides on specially scheduled days. You can call and make arrangements for personal rides.

Fees vary for that. Kathy House provides food at the groups rides. The menu varies: buffalo burgers, barbeque, hot dogs, steak, etc. You can brown bag it or purchase lunch from the hosts for a minimal price.

Even with large groups the rides move along at an average pace. Pete and Kathy who lead the rides try to hold waiting time to a minimum. The dinner meal is most often served somewhere on the trail, for example at the natural spring. Pete and Kathy did a lot of work on this area. They added natural rock steps to the spring, put up hitching lines, and provided a chemical toilet.

Rules and Responsibilities:

Please call and cancel at least by the night before the ride if you can't come. This helps prevent waste of time, patience, and food. Please be courteous to the ride host and the other riders.

For More Information:

The Houses plan a ride a month. **CALL** for reservations.
Evenings 405-398-4643
Days 405-553-4873

McGee Creek
Natural Scenic Recreation Horse Trails

Overview:

The land in the natural scenic recreation area near McGee State Park has been preserved much as it was when the first riders saw it. Perhaps, Captain Randolph B. Marcy was one of those first riders. He explored much of southeastern Oklahoma and wrote the first rail riders guide, *The Prairie Traveler* (1859).

The eight thousand nine hundred acres which has been set aside has four specific concepts: a quiet water zone, a wilderness-type recreation experience, non-motorized activities, and preservation of natural and cultural resources.

Location of the Trail:

From Antlers, Oklahoma take Hwy. 3 west about five miles. Turn north or right at the Centerpoint Grocery Store. At this turn you will see two state signs. One says continue straight ahead on Hwy. 3 to McGee State Park. **Don't**. The other sign says turn right and drive 13 miles to McGee Creek Recreation Area. The recreation area is where the horse trails are. As you

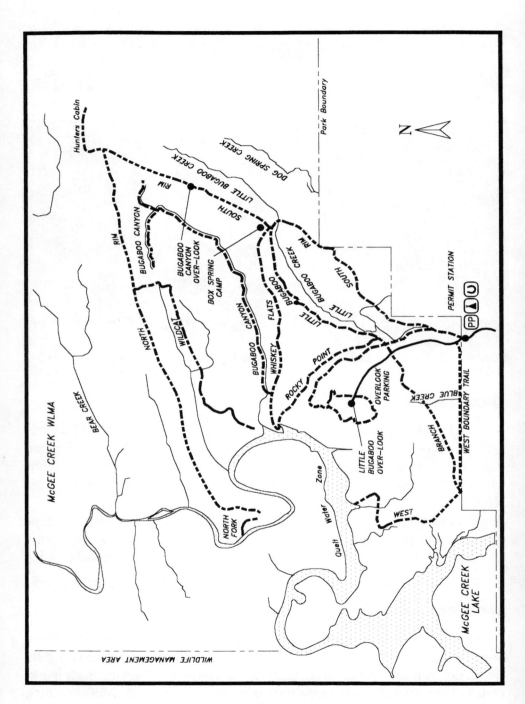

McGee Creek Recreation Area

approach the permit station you will see a privately owned equestrian campground on the left. These are the only facilities on this side of the lake.

Camp Facilities Summary:

Type: Private; day use or overnight camping.
Fees: Unknown
Electric: None
Showers: Yes
Water: none

Trail Summary:

Type: Public, use by permit.
Terrain: Rough woods, unforgiving black jack oak; mostly two track trail around the rim of a canyon. The trails change according to where the rangers think horses should and should not go. Do not ride in closed areas.
Difficulty: Moderately difficult. This can be a difficult area if you get off the designated trail. Steep ups and downs and thick underbrush. There are some boggy areas in the bottoms near the lake.
Length: 10 miles out and back if you ride the two rim trails.
Trail Markers: Multi-use trails, primarily old logging roads are designated with a square on a white marker. Hiker/biker trails are designed with a circle on a yellow marker and the hiker only/nature trails are marked with a diamond on a blue marker.

Trail Notes:

The black top access road to this recreation area is pretty good, but there are some dips that sure can make your trailer buck if you don't slow down before you hit them. This is more of problem when you are going toward the recreation area than when you are coming back.

When the author visited this trail the campground was so new it was still under construction. The parking pads were pea gravel back-ins. They were pretty high and narrow but a little time and some use will begin to level them out more. You can see the permit office from the equestrian camp. It is just down the road on the right. A person or group must get a permit to enter the area. The area is day use only for equestrians.

The beginning of the horse and mule trails are just behind the office. When you come to the McGee Creek sign in front of the office, turn right and follow the little road. Once you have passed the rangers house look across the yard. You will see a waist high narrow brown sign with white letters. This where the trails begin. Don't count too much on markers anywhere but at intersections.

The North and South Rim trails run along the crest of Bugaboo Canyon. Spaces in the black jack oaks let you see the horizon miles away. In many sections the rocks aren't bad so it can be a fun place for an easy canter.

Trail Rules:

Stay on the trails.
Travel at a safe speed.
Slow to a walk when approaching or overtaking other trail users.
Walking, trotting, and slow cantering are appropriate on horse trails.
Horses have the right-of-way over all other users.
Do not ride on the trail when it is muddy. Deep hoof ruts are difficult to repair and make the trail hazardous for other users.
Horses may not be tethered to trees or structures.

Nearest Services:

Groceries, feed, veterinary and health care can be found in Antlers approximately 18 miles away. Picnic supplies can be purchased at the Centerpoint Grocery on Hwy 3.

For more information:

405-889-5822

Robbers Cave Equestrian Trails

Overview:

The legends of Robbers Cave began as early as the 1700's with French trappers who used the shelter to store their trade provisions. Later the area was used by both the the North and South during the Civil War. However, the most infamous user of this cave has to be Belle Star.

Belle used the caves in the area to hide many of her ruthless friends who were continually sought by the law. Part of the James gang was besieged by US Marshalls in Robbers Cave for the better part of two days. One outlaw was killed and others were captured after they were smoked out. To Oklahoma trail riders, this cave is important because it is within the boundary of the oldest public marked horse trail in the state. The trail was established in 1980 and members of Oklahoma Equestrian Trail Riders Association (OETRA) have maintained these trails since 1982.

Location of the trail:

Robbers Cave State park is located five miles north of Wilburton or 12

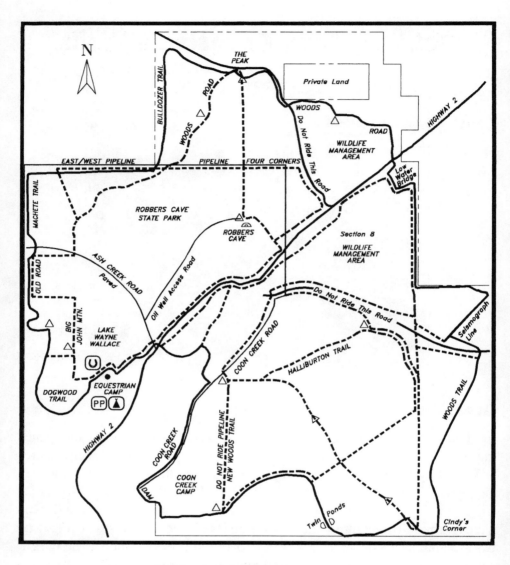

Robbers Cave Equestrian Trails

miles south of Quinton on Hwy 2 in southeastern Oklahoma. The equestrian camp is on a paved park road which parrellels the highway on the west side. It is one-half mile north of the park cafe & swimming pool. Signs announcing Equestrian camp mark the way.

Camp Facilities Summary:

Type: Day use or overnight camping.
Fees: $8.00 per day if you park on a pad with electric (even if you don't plug in). $2.00 additional if you use the electrical service. $6.00 a day for other sites. 25 sites are available.
Electric: Yes
Restroom: Yes, flush toilets
Showers: Yes, hot water
Water: Yes for both people and horses.

Trail Summary:

Type: Public use fee for camping only.
Terrain: Mountainous, rocky, lots of Pines, creek crossings, and beautiful mountian views.
Difficulty: Moderate
Length: The trails are loop type trails. All loops vary in length. Check map for lengths.
Trail markers: Markers on trees
Trail Maps: Yes, check with State Park Office.

Trail Notes:

These trails are the oldest public horse trails in the state of Oklahoma. They are maintained by OETRA. Oklahoma trail riders have come up with an adopt a section of the trail policy. Certain riders are responsible for certain sections of the trail. This seems to be working pretty well. The camp facilities are good. The trails vary in their difficulty. All the trails are beautiful. Because the trails crisscross in some places it is easy to set up short or long rides.

Camp Rules and Responsibilities:

Do not tie horses or picket lines to trees.
No Dogs allowed in camp.

You are responsible for your own safety at all times.
Absolutely no beer or alcoholic drinks on the trail.
Bag manure and hay. Leave it *near* NOT In the trash cans.
RVs requiring use of a generator motor will please park on extreme south end of campgrounds. Be considerate of your neighbors.

Nearest Services:

Gas, Groceries, feed or veterinary care can be found as close in Wilburton (five miles).

For More Information:

Robbers Cave State Park
P.O. Box 9
Wilburton, OK 74578
918-465-2565

Sportsman Lake Equestrian Trails

Overview:

From a Mekusudy Indian Mission, to a settlement known as "Tidmore", to a population of over 35,000 during the oil boom, Seminole was a community with growing pains. Vice and corruption came with the oil boom. Bootlegging, hijacking, and brawling were common occurrences. But the city recovered from the problems associated with the development of the Greater Seminole Oil Field. Even though Fixico No. 1 which started it all, no longer pumps, there is a replica of the rig in the city Municipal Park. Riding on horse trails throughout the area, one finds trails that wander through or around vintage pieces of drilling equipment left as memories of the great boom times.

Location of the Trail:

From Seminole take Hwy 9 east four miles. Turn right at the Texaco store and continue for two miles. Turn left on EW 124 at the Sportsman's Lake sign. Follow this blacktop a mile or so, then cross a cattle guard. Take the first left on a dirt or gravel road. Follow the signs to the parking area.

Camp Facilities Summary:

Type: Day use. (Local riders are currently working on permission to camp here.)

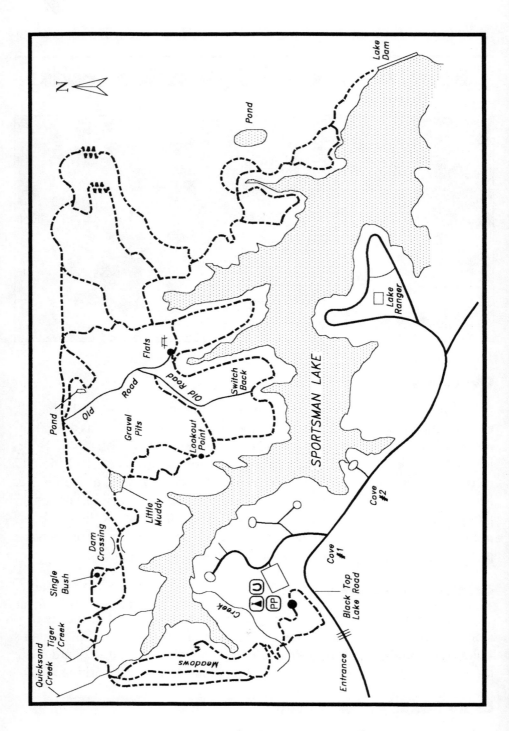

Sportsman Lake Equestrian Trails

Fee: $2.00 an animal per day or $30.00 a year.
Electric: None
Restrooms: None
Showers: None
Water: None

Trail Summary:

Type: Public; day use
Terrain: Trees, woods, good single track trails. A variety of terrain with a couple of creek crossings.
Difficulty: Easy to moderate
Length: 15 miles. Out and back with some different loops. You can not ride around the lake.
Trail Markers: Ribbons and squares or circles nailed on trees.
Trail Maps: No specific maps at this time.

Trail Notes:

Sportsman's Lake trails are diverse, ranging in difficulty from very easy to challenging.

The trail traverses rough rock outcroppings and passes through small quiet valleys. Creek crossing provide water breaks for the horses. Mid-way through the ride a picnic tables waits under a big shade tree. The table and benches were provided by the Oklahoma Equestrian Trail Riders Association. Much of the trail is sandy but there is enough rock that shoes are highly recommended.

As is true on any trail watch the creek crossing during wet weather.

Nearest Services:

Veterinary, gas, food, and feed and health care can be found in Seminole, approximately six miles. Picnic supplies can be found at the Texaco store at the corner of Hwy 9.

For more information:

Sportsman Lake
Rt. 2, Box 194T
Seminole, OK 74868
405-257-3600

Stanley Draper Lake Horse Trail

Overview:

This is a metropolitan trail with a country flavor. When you look at the map you would swear this trail was located in downtown Del City. It might very well be but when you are out there riding you hardly notice it. This is a trail many people in the state ignore because of its urban location. If you talk to a local rider you will get an entirely different impression, most of them think it is a great place to ride.

Location of the Trail:

Between Midwest Blvd and Post Rd. It stretches from SE 74th to SE 134th in Oklahoma City. Open year round from 5am to 11pm.

Camp Facilities Summary:

Type: Day use
Fees: None
Electric: None
Restroom: None
Showers: None
Water: None

Trail Summary:

Type: Public use.
Terrain: Some trees, woods, and flat. Most of the trail parallels the lake shore.
Difficulty: Easy.
Length: Approximately 28 miles.
Trail markers: Trails are not marked but they are used enough your can tell where to go in most cases.
Trail Maps: None.

Trail Notes:

Horse people who live in the area around Stanley Draper Lake use the trail to exercise their horses, to condition the horses for other riding purposes and for pleasure. The trails are easy and fairly level. These are good trails for cantering.

Camp Rules and Responsibilities:

Do not tie horses to trees.
Be sure to stay on the trail
Bag manure and old hay and take it home with you
No loose or hobbled horses

Nearest Services:

Del City, Moore, or Midwest City

For More Information:

405-799-0870

Talimena Horse Trails

Overview:

Talimena State Park is located at the gateway to the Ouachita National Forest in Oklahoma. The park is in the heart of a pine and hardwood forest. While the park is best known as the beginning of the 192 mile Ouachita National Recreation Trail for hikers, it is an excellent camp ground and jumping off point for equestrians.

Location of the Trail:

From the junction of 270 and 271 follow 271 south into the Winding Stair Mountains. The park, located on the east side of the highway, is small as state parks go. To find the parking area, go past the ranger office, take a right and proceed through the RV camp to the back where you will see a play area. As you approach the children's swing set turn between the two short brown posts onto the grass and make a sharp right around the sand pit that is built under the swings. You have to watch your space pretty carefully if you are pulling a long rig. Circle and pull between the two play areas and head for the trees at the back of the park. You will be able to see where other trailers have been backing in. You may highline or tie to your trailer. Do not tie directly to trees. If you use trees, highline with tree savers.

Camp Facilities Summary:

Type: Public; day use and overnight camping.
Fees: Yes; call for current information.
Electric: It is available if you want it.
Rest rooms: Yes with flush toilets
Showers: Yes
Water: Yes, for people and animals

Trail Summary:

Type: Public: Equestrian and hikers
Terrain: Mountainous and rocky
Difficulty: Mostly difficult
Length: Set your own
Trail Markers: Basically none at the time of printing

Trail Notes:

From this campsite you can ride to Cedar Lake, Billy Creek, and Horse Pen, that is if you like a challenge. There are no marked trails yet but they are in the process. It is an all day ride to Cedar Lake and unless you have been there before you better have a rider familiar with the area or be good at reading maps and a compass. Most of the trails are old logging roads. There is also an old military road that cuts through this area.

Trails through here are so beautiful that I feel sure more and more people will want to ride in the area.

Rules and Regulations:

Don't drink from streams or ponds.
Use rocky areas to cross steams and wet areas.
Scatter hay and manure when camping along the trail.

Use tree saver straps. Don't tie directly to trees.
Pack it in...Pack it out.

Nearest Services:

Services to this area are limited. Talihina is the closest but that would be mostly for gas, groceries and feed. Wilburton and then McAlister would be the next two largest towns where you might find hospital and vet services.

For More Information:

Choctaw Ranger District
HC 64, Box 3467
Heavener, OK 74937
918-653-2991

Beware of Ornery Stuff on the Trail or How to Avoid Encounters that Sting, Itch, or Bite.

Yellowjackets, You and Your Horse

A yellowjacket is the common name for several different species of wasps that often occur on wooded trails. They live in colonies housed in nests. Some species attach the nest to trees, shrubs or buildings. But the major enemy of the trail rider is the yellowjacket that constructs its nest underground. Nests are constructed from a paper substance made by the insect when they chew plant fibers. When this pulp is spread out it dries to form paper. The inner core of the nest is a series of horizontal combs which contain many six-sided cells all surrounded by sheets of paper. These structures can be found in rotten logs, rodent holes, or any natural crevice. They are often covered with a thin layer of dead leaves.

While most yellowjackets are attracted to sweet foods such as fruit, cookies and soft drinks, the flitty critters that hang around camp are not the ones that cause rider's nightmares. It's those villainous creatures that lie in wait on the trail. The ones that come out of holes that no ones sees and swarm around about the third or fourth horse in line. It is these that strike terror in the heart of the even the most fearless rider.

Yellowjackets defend themselves by delivering a powerful sting which causes pain, swelling and itching. Certain people and horses who are allergic can suffer serious medical complications from such contact.

Yellowjackets sting when they sense a threat to themselves or their colonies. Those near the nest will attack anything that disturbs the ground or passes close by.

A rider usually has three options when attacked by yellowjackets—dismount, get bucked off or run for it. In this case making a run for it is your best bet if you can control your mount so you don't get thrown off in the process. It is impossible to ask a horse or mule to stand still while they are being repeatedly stung. Get away as quickly as possible. Yellowjackets seldom go more than 50 yards from their nest. The minute you are away from the area, if you know for sure your horse has been stung, dismount and look for yellowjackets still clinging to your horse. These stubborn insects sometimes have to be knocked with your hat or gloves.

If you are stung and the stinger remains in your skin, you can usually remove it by scraping from the side with your fingernail. Apply cold water or ice in a wet cloth. Do not drink alcohol.

People who are highly allergic to the venom may develop serious medical problems. If you have any of the following symptoms seek help immediately. Hives, widespread swelling of limbs, painful joints, wheezing, shortness of breath, faintness, dizziness, vomiting, abdominal cramps, nasal discharge or tightening of the throat.

If you are severely allergic to such bites you might consider carrying a cell phone or two-way radio for such emergencies.

Poisonous Snakes

There are rattlesnakes, copperheads, and water moccasins in Oklahoma. In fact there are some locations in Oklahoma that are famous for the number of rattlesnakes they can produce. However, poisonous snakes are seldom a problem if treated with respect. Watch your step, carry a flash light if you must move around after dark on hot summer nights. Mind your own business and most of the time the snakes will avoid you.

Be particularly aware around late evening camp fires. Some copperheads are attracted by the warmth and bright light. They have been known to coil up and rest under unsuspecting rider's lawn chairs. Most snakes will not strike unless provoked. When you gather wood for a fire watch where you reach and where you step. Keep a snake bite kit available.

In Case of Snake Bite

The most important step in first aid for snakebite is to get the victim to the hospital as quickly as possible. Calm the victim and keep them in a lying position, if possible. Immobilize the bitten extremity and keep it at or below heart level. If you are within a 4 or 5 hour drive to a hospital no further first aid is necessary.

Additional considerations.
- Identify the snake.
- Clean the bite area.
- Do not give the victim alcohol, sedatives, aspirin, or any medicine containing aspirin.
- Keep a snakebite kit accessible for all outings.
- It is not recommended that cold compresses, ice, dry ice, chemical ice packs, spray refrigerants, or other methods of cold therapy be used in the first aid treatment of snakebite.
- Give fluids and anticipate shock.

Chiggers

Chiggers are tiny little red insects that lives on southern grass and weeds. These little creatures particularly like to live on plants that are not mowed frequently. The chigger is an itchy, irritating problem once they are on your skin.

There isn't any foolproof way to stop chiggers. Many people use a large number of home remedies. One of the best methods of prevention is to spray your pant legs, boot tops, and shirt sleeves with an insect repellent before you ever get exposed. Other people swear by vitamin B1. They say taking a B1 tablet before you go out will minimize the number of ticks and chiggers you get. You have to be your own judge in these matters.

Poison Oak, Ivy and Sumac

Poison oak, ivy and sumac are found in almost all areas of the United States. It seems to me this stuff grows best along horse trails and in the best places to stop for lunch. If you are allergic, learn to recognize the plant. If you get it on your skin or clothes, try to keep your hands away from your eyes and nose. If you can, bath within 12 hours of exposure you can often prevent an outbreak. Be aware that if you are very allergic you can get it from your dog, who runs through it, or from your horses muzzle or their legs after they walk through it. Also be careful what you choose to burn in your camp fire. Burning poison oak or ivy stems or leaves can also cause exposure.

Symptoms of plant poisoning are a rash or reddening of the skin with itching and swelling, often blisters appear. The best treatment if you contact the plant is immediate washing with strong soap. There are many over-the-counter products that help releave the itch.

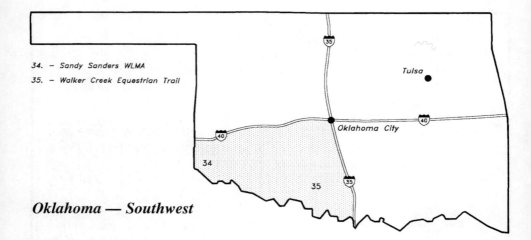

Oklahoma — Southwest

34. – Sandy Sanders WLMA
35. – Walker Creek Equestrian Trail

Sandy Sanders Wildlife Management Area

Overview:

The history of this area is cattle and cowboys. Much of land in Sanders WLMA and the surrounding community began as part of Texas in 1880. Southwest Oklahoma is a vast region of rugged natural beauty. It is rugged when riding because you have to dodge cactus and prickly bushes. But the quiet natural beauty whispers to horseman's soul.

Location of the Riding Area:

To get to Sandy Sanders WLMA take Hwy 30 south from Erick. You will see a sign announcing the WLMA. The entrance is on the east side of the road. You will see an old cattle shed, wind mill and stock tank. There is plenty of room to turn your rig around and plenty of room to get off the road while saddling up. There is a bulletin board with maps and rules.

Camp Facilities Summary:

Type: None
Fees: None

Electric: None
Rest rooms: None
Showers: None
Water: None

Trail Summary:

Type: Public; day use
Terrain: Grassland pasture; low hills; steep gullies and arroyos; a few low trees, an abundance of cactus.
Difficulty: Easy, moderate, difficult. Set your own difficulty level.
Length: Choose your own. There are no marked trails. Set your own time.
Trail Markers: None

Trail Notes:

The riding area is subject to all the rules that apply to riding on Oklahoma WLM land. Sometimes you have to contact the individual biologists that over see that particular area to get the final word on when you can ride there. Most of the time these areas are open except from September 15 to the end of deer gun season. The land is open except for a fence here and there. You can choose to ride the roads that network across the area or you can just take off cross country riding cattle trails. Near the highway you have to be alert if you want avoid the cactus. I thought at first the cactus was going to take the pleasure out of the ride but as I got away from the highway the cactus began to diminish.

The land looks like many western moving you have seen with cowboys and cow country. You ride up on hills and see Herefords dotting the land scape. You might expect to see the big Conestoga wagons lumbering across the plains in front of you. In some places grass was growing chest high on my mule. Ruth loved it because she could easily grab quick bites as we walked.

This land is made unique by the cattle trails that lead to rocky arroyos, short box canyons and springs. A combination of Louis L'Amour and Zane Grey, this country just seems to call to riders. There is just enough devil in it to keep it interesting.

Nearest Services:

Sandy Sanders WLMA is sandwiched between Erick and Mangum. It depends on which side you come in from which town would be the closest. Either town can provide you with feed, food and gas.

For More Information:

Oklahoma Dept. Of Wildlife Conservation
1801 N. Lincoln
P.O. Box 53465
Oklahoma City, OK 73105
405- 521-3851

Walker Creek Equestrian Trail

Overview:

With a name like Waurika meaning "good water" in Native American, it is not surprising to find a horse trail around a lake. This area has a long history for both cowboys and Native Americans. The main route of the Chishom Trail passed within five miles of Waurika. Wranglers moving large cattle herds to the north chose this rich grassland to fatten their cattle during a drive.

The land which was actually part of the Kiowa-Comanche reservation was opened to white settlement by land lottery in 1901. The town still exploits it local pest the rattlesnake. Waurika hosts a rattlesnake hunt once a year when thousands come to comb the surrounding countryside for the scary, poisonous reptile.

Location of the Trail:

Walker Creek trailhead is located one mile north of the Wichita Ridge Park on the east side of the road. This is a blacktop county road that runs between Hastings and Corum. The sign on the roads will say Walker Creek Nature Trail.

Camp Facilities Summary:

Type: Day use; overnight camping is not allowed on the trail, but an adjacent primitive area is available.
Fees: None
Electric: None
Restroom: None
Showers: None
Water: None

Trail Summary:

Type: Public use
Terrain: Flat, open pastures, mixed oak forest on the creek bottoms. No rocks. Pretty views of the lake. Three primitive creek crossings. One long bridge to cross if you ride the whole loop.
Difficulty: Easy.
Length: 13 miles.
Trail Markers: This trail is mainly marked by mowing biannually and by the traffic patterns. There are a few Karsonite or wooden markers at intersections or road crossings. With the use of the map this is a pretty straight forward trail to ride.
Trail Maps: Yes, check with lake headquarters for latest information.

Trail Notes:

The trailer parking area is flat, graveled and bordered with a pipe fence. The fence is strong enough you can use it as a hitching rail. There is no shade on the lot but you can tie on the other side of the fence and in some shade when the sun is in the right direction. This is only a day use parking spot.

The trailhead is well marked with a sign near the gate. Other turns and intersections are marked with Karsonite posts that have a rider, hiker and arrow indicating the direction of travel.

The ground is sandy and great for galloping. The trail meanders through cottonwood and willow thickets that provide shade even on the hot days. Several sections of the trail are enhanced by sand plum bushes that provide a nice snack if you are riding during the season they are ripe.

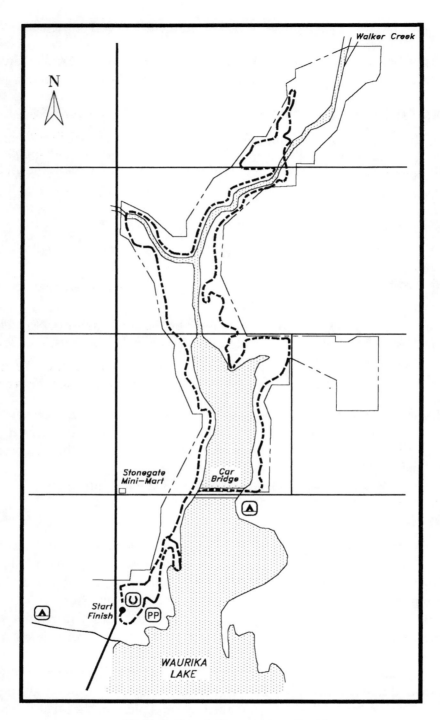

Walker Creek Equestrian Trail

Birds are abundant - quail, dove, plover, crow and owl. Other wildlife you might see include coyote, white-tail deer, wild turkey, cotton tailed rabbit, and fox squirrel.

Several residences along with frequent law enforcement patrols provide security for trail users and their vehicles. Because this area is also used by hunters, equestrians are not allowed to ride the trail from September 15 through the end of deer gun season. If you are unsure of the date contact the park office.

Camp Rules and Responsibilities:

Do not tie horses to trees.
Be sure to stay on marked trail
If you want to water your horse on shore areas watch for bogs.
Courtesy is the rule - in camp and on the trails.

Nearest Services:

Restaurant and convenience store less than one mile north of the trail head. Veterinary and health service in Waurika about seven miles south east.

For More Information:

U.S. Army Corps of Engineers
Waurika Project Office
P.O. Box 29
Waurika, OK 73573
405-963-2111

Additional Information

State Park Stables

What state parks offer in the way of trail riding varies according to the terrain and the amount of land that is available. Not all state parks have stables but those that do differ in rules, regulations, and costs. If you don't have a horse and want to rent one, check out all the details with the stable you plan to use. The following state parks had stables at the time this book went to print.

Beavers Bend Stables at Beaver Bend State Park

Visitors who choose guided horseback rides have the opportunity to see deer, beaver, mink, eastern wild turkey, fox, raccoon, and squirrels. There is over 3500 acres in Beavers Bend State park. The whole area is nestled in towering pines, oak and hickory where the Mountain Fork River runs wild.

Beavers Bend Resort Park
P.O. Box 10
Broken Bow, OK 74728
405-494-6300

Fountainhead Stables at Lake Eufaula in Fountainhead State Park

Located on 2800 acres that were once the hunting lands of the Osage Indian tribe. Fountainhead State Park offers the traveler many different outdoor opportunities. The park is adjacent to Lake Eufaula, Oklahoma's largest lake.

Fountainhead Stables offers guided rides by appointment. They also offer hay rides and chuck wagon cookouts. In addition they have a gift saddle shop that features western and Indian art by professional handicraftsmen. Call for reservations.

Fountainhead State Park
HC60 Box 1340
Checotah, OK 74426
918-689-9739

Murray Stables at Murray State Park

The Lake Murray area offers a variety of entertaining opportunities such as Arbuckle Wilderness, 77 foot Turner Falls, Historic Fort Washita, and Chickasaw National Recreation Area (see other listing). The stables offer guided horseback rides as well as hay rides. Call for more information.

Lake Murray Resort
Box 1329
Ardmore, Oklahoma 73402
405-223-6600

Roman Nose Stable at Roman Nose State Park

Five hundred and forty acres makes Roman Nose the smallest Oklahoma state park. But size does not diminish the recreational opportunities. This park has long been known for its rich Indian history. Long ago, Cheyenne and Arapaho tribes sought refuge in the canyon. Native trees include blackjacks, chestnuts, red cedars and cottonwoods. Though the buffalo is gone many other species of wild game still call the canyon home. Tours can be taken from horseback with the benefit of an interpretive guide. The stable trails wind through cedar and across the gypsum hills. Call for more information.

Roman Nose Resort Park
Box 61
Watonga, OK 73772
(405)623-7281

Texoma Park Riding Stables at Lake Texoma near Kingston

Lake Texoma is on the border between Texas and Oklahoma. 93,000 acres of water makes this resort a fishing and water recreation haven. But for those who prefer a more western flavor there is a riding stable. Call for more information.

Texoma State Park
P.O. Box 279
Kingston, OK 73439
405-564-2566

Little River Stables at Lake Thunderbird in Little River State Park

Thirteen miles east of Norman, Oklahoma on SH-9 Little River State Park is open year round. The park provides RV hookups, picnic areas, playgrounds, equestrian facilities. Call for information.

405-360-3572

Sequoyah Stables at Western Hills Guest Ranch in Sequoyah State Park

Sequoyah Stables have trails that travel across the famous land of the Cherokee Nation. There are 300 acres of open prairie and wooded trails. The park is 2800 acres within 50 minutes of Tulsa. To the north is the rugged foothills of the Boston Mountains and to the south lie the Cookson Hills. This is a great place to get a feeling of the old west. Call for more information.

Western Hills Guest Ranch
Box 509
Wagoner, Oklahoma 74477
918-772-2545

Guest Ranches

Coyote Hills Ranch

P.O. Box 99
Cheyenne, OK 73628
Phone: 405-497-3931
FAX: 405-497-2176

Location: Coyote Hills Ranch is located midway between Oklahoma City and Amarillo, Texas. Take Exit 20 off I-40 at Sayre, then US-283 north 28 miles to Cheyenne. Go west on SH-47 for 4 miles(watch for signs), 2 miles north and 2 miles west.

"Old West adventure with modern comforts."

Old West adventure, unrivaled rugged beauty and make yourself-at home hospitality describes a visit to this 480 acre vacation spot snuggled in at the edge of the Black Kettle National Grasslands of western Oklahoma. This place is classic old west complete with bunkhouse and tepees. The bunkhouse has 20 private rooms and baths and is furnished in rustic old west. A 7500foot social barn offers a dining room, dance floor, theater, library, sitting area with fireplace and trading post. Families or groups of any size are welcome. Ride a horse or hike along old cattle trails, sleep in an Indian tepee and savor tasty home style fare at a chuck wagon cookout. Share the fun and excitement of an Indian Pow Wow, cowboy poetry gatherings, and special weekend rides with a covered wagon. Call for reservations.

Allen Ranch

19600 S. Memorial
Bixby, OK 74008
Phone: 918-366-3010

Location:
    The Allen Ranch is located on Memorial south of 181st street south of Bixby, Oklahoma.

"Where the Pavement Ends and the West Begins."

The Allen Ranch near Bixby, is a working horse and cattle ranch, in addition to being a guest ranch. Open Tuesdays through Sundays year-round, the ranch experience includes a bunk house divided down the middle with cowboys on one side and cowgirls on the other. Each side includes thirty bunkbeds, heat, air conditioning, running water and separate bathroom facilities.

Guests are offered horseback riding, horsemanship training, trail drives, roping instructions, horse care & maintenance instruction, demonstrations on horse and equipment, fishing, archery, swimming. Call for information and reservations.

Read Ranch

Route 1, box 159
Chandler, OK 74834
405-258-2999
Open Year Round
closed on Mondays

Location:
　　Take old Route 66 west out of Chandler, Oklahoma, 4.5 miles and turn north for 3 miles.

"Experience the Best of the Old West"

The Read Ranch offers a distinctive western atmosphere: trail rides, hay wagon rides, petting zoo, pony rides, breakfast trail rides, chuck wagon suppers, overnight camp-outs, RV & tent campsites with hook ups and dump station, gift shop, snack bar, full moon trail rides, horse and buggy rental, and many special occasion events. Call for latest information.

Western Hills Guest Ranch

Box 509
Wagoner, Oklahoma 74477
918-772-2545
1-800-654-8240

Location:
East of Wagnor on Highway 51 just across the Fort Gibson bridge.

"There's No Limit To Our Hospitality"

The setting is a peninsula in the 2800 acre Sequoyah State Park on 19,000 acre fort Gibson Lake. The ranch has 101 rooms which sleep up to four people, pool side cabanas, and specialty theme suites. Dining is always a special event whether in the Calico Crossing restaurant or during one of the popular chuck wagon cookouts or haywagon barbecues. Trail rides parallel the lake shore. Call for reservations.

There are many other Guest and Dude Ranches in Oklahoma. For more information check with the Tourism Department.

About Our Illustrator

Our illustrations have been done for us by artist-illustrator, Becky Garner. Becky teaches art for the public schools in Ardmore, Oklahoma where she lives with her husband Bob, 2 cats, 2 dogs, and 2 mules.

Ms. Garner holds 2 master's degrees, 13 teaching certifications and has taught in public and private schools from elementary through graduate levels. As a working artist her recent work focuses on portraits of children and animals. In addition to her horse and mule portraits she works with champion show dogs.

Betty Robinson

About the Author

Betty Robinson has been passionate about horses since early childhood. Growing up in Oklahoma she's spent hours riding, training and showing horses. Later in life as she narrowed her interests to trail riding she became equally passionate about the mule.

Today Betty has authored a book about trail riding in her adopted state of Arkansas, *Guide to Arkansas Horse Trails*. She also produced, wrote and filmed a video to accompany the Arkansas guide, *Destination Arkansas: Ride the Natural State*. The *Horse Trails of Oklahoma* book and the video, *Destination Oklahoma: Riding the Sooner State* are further expressions of her love for trail riding.

An avid outdoors-person, Betty is a active member of Backcountry Horsemen of America and the National Saddle Mule Association, and all their state and regional affiliates.

TRAIL RIDER'S BOOK SHELF

from **Tack 'N Trails USA**
P.O. Box 255
London, AR 72847-0255

To Order Books and Videos by Betty Robinson
use this form (or fax it to 501-293-3253)

Quantity	Item	Price	Total
_____	*A Guide to Arkansas Horse Trails* 100 pages	$12.95	_____
_____	*Destination Arkansas: Ride the Natural State* VHS 25 minutes	$19.95	_____
_____	*Horse Trails of Oklahoma*	$16.95	_____
_____	*Destination Oklahoma: Ride the Sooner State* VHS 45 minutes	$24.95	_____

Prices subject to change. Orders shipped *U.S.P.S. or U.P.S*

Shipping (US funds): $2.50 for first item, $1.00 for additional items; Canada, $4.75 for first item, $2.00 each additional item; All other countries, $8.00 for first item, $3.00 each additional _____

Arkansas residents please add 5.5% sales tax _____

Total Amount _____

Method of Payment:
☐ check ☐ money order ☐ Visa ☐ MasterCard ☐ Discover

Credit Card Number _____ Ex. Date _____

Telephone Number_____